Praise for

UNCOMPLICATED MARKETING

"No matter what industry you're in, this engaging book has valuable marketing insights, concepts, and ideas that can be easily implemented. A must-read for every business owner and marketer."

— Laura DiFilippo
President, DiFilippo's Service Company

"*Uncomplicated Marketing* is packed full of helpful advice that's certain to benefit anyone who is interested in marketing their business!"

— Kelly VanVleet
Marketing Director, VanVleet Insurance

"Avery Manko lays out a master business marketing plan that is efficient, cost effective, and, most importantly, makes growing your business fun."

— Dr. Steven R. Karp
Chiropractic Physician, Stateline Chiropractic

UNCOMPLICATED MARKETING

UNCOMPLICATED MARKETING

A NO-NONSENSE GUIDE TO GROWING YOUR BUSINESS USING PROMOTIONAL PRODUCTS

Avery Manko

Alpharetta, GA

ISBN: 978-1-63183-667-1 - Paperback
eISBN: 978-1-63183-668-8 - ePub
eISBN: 978-1-63183-669-5 - mobi

Printed in the United States of America   1 1 2 0 1 9

⊗This paper meets the requirements of ANSI/NISO Z39.48-1992 (Permanence of Paper)

To Diana . . .
my wife, my best friend, and my business partner

CONTENTS

ACKNOWLEDGMENTS

I'd like to thank my friends and customers who participated in my survey in the summer of 2018. The data gathered was so helpful. I also received useful feedback regarding the title and cover design.

Thank you to my customers who allowed me to share their examples of how they used promotional products.

My friend Jody Gray helped me with some editing—thanks, buddy!

Moumita Das at Promotional Products Association International answered all the questions I had about the results of their research.

I love the cover Boni Buchanan designed. Thank you, Boni.

Thank you to a friend, mentor, and prolific writer, Ken Dooley. When I put my hands on a keyboard to write anything, I always ask myself, How would Ken say this?

My wife, Diana, deserves some sort of medal.

During the year it took me to write this, I shirked household chores and drove her nuts bouncing ideas off her about the content of this book. Regardless, she was so supportive of my efforts. She did a lot of editing, too.

DEAR MARKETER . . .

In August of 1996, I purchased a new car from a local dealership. I remember the salesperson: a man named Bill "M." Since that day, I've purchased five other vehicles, and I cannot for the life of me recall the names of the other salespeople who sold me those cars.

But I remember Bill.

Why do I remember Bill after all these years? Well, a few days after I purchased the vehicle, a small box was delivered to me by the US Post Office. Naturally, I opened it (wouldn't you?) and inside was a handwritten thank-you note and an inexpensive travel mug featuring the dealership's name and some contact information. Even though I had many sample mugs given to me by my promotional products suppliers, I liked using the mug Bill gave me. I liked Bill and I liked my new car, and there was a connection between me, Bill, and the car. The mug faithfully did its job delivering Bill's marketing message until it eventually disappeared, but Bill's name has stuck in my head ever since.

This example demonstrates why promotional products are the easiest, most cost effective, and most uncomplicated way to market a business. Think about it—someone at the dealership purchased some inexpensive imprinted travel mugs, and when Bill sold that car to me, a mug was boxed up, Bill's handwritten thank-you note was placed inside, and the box was addressed and sent to me. In today's dollars, Bill's marketing couldn't have cost much more than ten dollars (mug, box, thank-you note, and postage). It didn't take sophisticated planning or a lot of money, and he didn't hire any consultants or marketing firms. All it took was some gumption, some creativity, a small amount of money, and a little bit of time.

The big idea is that Bill didn't waste big bucks marketing to the universe. Instead, he invested a small portion of his already earned commission marketing directly to me, a qualified buyer who had bought from him and who would need to buy another car in the future. When he invested his marketing money in me, he invested in continuing a relationship with the hopes that I buy more cars from him or refer him to my friends and family.

The mug was intended to create another opportunity for him to sell me a car at a later date. Does ten dollars sound like a lot of money to spend on marketing if I come back to him to buy another car, or I refer others to him? I don't think so! Sending me the mug didn't guarantee Bill a future sale, but it could help facilitate one. Marketing has many roles, but one of them is to create an opportunity for a future sale. It would be up to Bill to close that deal. If Bill hadn't sent me that mug, I may have forgotten his name, just like the other five salespeople, and he would have most likely never had another potential sale with me.

This leads me to the reason why I wrote this book.

I love promotional products. I think they're the best way to market a business for a variety of reasons, which I will discuss in this book. Despite my opinion, promotional products continue to receive little respect from the marketing community. Some people call them "trinkets and trash" or "tchotchkes" or "swag." They are often an afterthought in the plans of some marketers. This is both a shame and shortsighted. I'm hoping this book will prove that promotional products are a truly powerful marketing medium.

Over the years, I've helped thousands of businesspeople make smart choices about marketing and promotional products. If I could sum up the conversations I've had with customers and prospects regarding promotional products, here's what they really want to know:

1. Why should I buy promotional products?
2. What promotional products should I buy?
3. How do I use them effectively?

I believe effective marketing doesn't need to be complex or expensive, and it's a lot easier than you think. You can do (notice the verb "do") great marketing on your own without the help or expense of consultants, marketing firms, or complicated and confusing marketing software. In the pages that follow, you'll find valuable information about promotional products and some simple ways you can immediately use them to market your business. While promotional products can be used for many purposes, from employee safety and recognition programs to branding and promotion, this book focuses only on the latter. Additionally, there are many ways to use promotional products to market a business. Some of these programs can be quite complex, utilizing custom-made items and packaging, but most businesspeople don't have the money, time, or expertise to create these promotions. Instead, this book centers on the simple, easy-to-deploy marketing ideas.

You may have noticed this book is short. This is intentional. This book is intended for business owners, entrepreneurs, and folks who are responsible for marketing a business or organization. These folks have a lot on their plate, and for this reason, I wanted this book to be as brief as possible.

After reading this book, you will be able to repurpose the ideas found within to help you make better marketing choices, generate and convert more leads, increase your average sale, increase the amount of transactions with each customer, and increase customer retention.

CHAPTER 1

WHY YOU SHOULD USE PROMOTIONAL PRODUCTS TO MARKET YOUR BUSINESS

Set it and forget it.

—Ron Popeil

I fell into the promotional products business in February of 1990, and aside from a brief detour in the late '90s, I've been in the industry my entire career. I've been witness to many changes in the industry, including the many disruptions in the marketing world like email marketing, digital marketing, and social media marketing. Marketing tools such as customer relationship management software (CRM software) and marketing automation programs have allowed marketers to be so much more efficient and effective. These mediums and tools are truly game changers, but as marketing has evolved to take advantage of greater and more sophisticated technologies, its task has become more and more complex. If you're like most marketers, you want to take advantage of the new technologies and use them to their fullest capabilities. In fact, you should be using them, otherwise your competitors might just eat your lunch. This forces you to figure out and implement these marketing wonders on your own or hire well-paid specialists to do the work for you. You have a choice between spending some big bucks hiring experts and hoping they're doing it correctly, or spending a lot of time and effort learning how to use the technology and managing it yourself. Have you ever tried to set up and manage a pay-per-click campaign? How about marketing automation software? What do you know about search engine optimization (SEO)? It's a confusing, frustrating, and time-consuming undertaking that requires expertise and dedication just to keep up with the constant changes. Do you have time and energy for that?

As a marketer, you have many marketing mediums at your disposal, but you're almost forced to use digital marketing to compete in today's world. Can you really market a business today without a website? Probably not. Do you have time to become a search engine optimization expert and attempt to tame the algorithms of the search engines? Again, probably not. Do you have time to become an expert on pay-per-click advertising, mobile advertising, marketing automation, click funnels, email marketing, social media marketing, landing pages, and so on, all while keeping up with the changes and managing it all while you're running a business? Do you have time to write blogs rich with keywords that are irresistible to search engines? Yet again, probably not. If you want to use digital marketing to market your business, you have two choices: do the work yourself or hire someone to do it for you. Either way, good luck. I hope you have time, patience, and money.

Despite its complexity, the demand for digital marketing is growing, while traditional marketing mediums are becoming increasingly irrelevant and ineffective. Have you noticed how thin the Yellow Pages are? Does anyone actually use them? The Yellow Pages in my area used to be an 8.5x11 book about three inches thick. Now it's 6x9 and less than one inch thick. Magazines are thinner, too, and they seem to have more ads than actual content. Who wants a magazine filled only with ads? Personally, I only listen to the radio when I'm in my car, and I rarely hear radio ads. The reason I don't hear them is that I change the station or use the mute button on my steering wheel (I love that feature). Maybe you do too. You don't wish for more TV ads, do you? I mute them or change the channel just like I do when I listen to the radio in my car. In fact, many of us pay for services like Netflix and Amazon Prime in order to avoid commercials. As far as newspapers, they're a dinosaur! Many of us get the news online. I've always been a fan of direct mail, but it can be pretty costly and requires accurate mailing lists and multiple mailings, otherwise you'll waste a ton of money. Outdoor advertising can be effective, but it's not very targeted. Do I even need to mention telemarketing? Not only are there legal restrictions, but everyone has caller ID, so who actually answers their phone anymore? Some of these mediums can be inexpensive when evaluated on a cost-per-one-thousand-impressions basis, but not everyone who comes in contact with this marketing pays attention to it or is a qualified prospect. Marketers need to factor in the cost of that wasted advertising money to get a better idea of the actual cost of their advertising. This fact alone makes these seemingly inexpensive, low-cost-per-thousand-impression marketing mediums actually pretty expensive in the long run.

I don't intend to knock these mediums—in fact, they need to be part of your overall marketing strategy—but they all have serious downsides. In my opinion, the biggest drawback of traditional marketing mediums is that they are not as efficient at targeting and keeping in touch with the ideal prospect or customer as digital marketing. I'm sure you'll agree that we don't turn to the Yellow Pages any longer; we use our phone or computer to search for just about anything we can think of buying. The Big Tech companies are happy to help us find whatever we need, which gives them the opportunity to collect so much of our personal data that they, for a price, can sell and efficiently deliver a marketing message to the most narrowly defined target market. This highly targeted marketing is the simple reason why traditional mediums are floundering while digital marketing is rising.

Digital marketing is amazing, and it's revolutionized the way businesses can market their products and services. However, it, too, has some downsides. In addition to being complicated, digital marketing can be really annoying. As a consumer, I'm sure you don't sit in front of your computer and hope to encounter another pop-up or banner ad. Don't you just love YouTube's countdown clock? It lets you know how much of your time they'll waste before letting you watch what you want to see in the first place. Do you block pop-up ads like a lot of other people do? Is your email account jammed with email marketing? Mine is. Do you ignore or unsubscribe from unwanted emails? I do that too.

Digital marketing is highly targeted and is great for marketers who understand it and can afford it, but as consumers, are we really happy with it? Do you really feel comfortable clicking on a pop-up ad or banner ad? I'm always hesitant to do it, but when I do, I always wonder what information of mine is being collected and what will happen to it. And after clicking on a pop-up or banner ad, I expect to dislike what Big Tech will do next: some marketer will start to follow me around the internet like a stalker. Like it or not, the data collection by Big Tech is ever-present in our lives, which is a cost we as consumers incur in order to enjoy the conveniences Big Tech offers. How does that make you feel? If you use digital marketing to market your business, do you think at least some of your customers feel the same way?

Case in point: One Sunday morning, I logged into Facebook and saw a post from my friend Ronnie. Here it is word for word:

> Was just browsing mattresses on Amazon and now my feed is flooded with mattresses….so creepy!!

Here are the comments she received:

> Respondent 1: Yup same thing here with backpacking gear.

> Respondent 2: That's how cookies work lol.

> Respondent 3: It's just a programming tactic reading your recent browser history to give you ads specific to your searches.

> Respondent 4: It gets way more sinister than that. That's a simple cookie. Walked into a store to use the bathroom and came out. Within a minute, I was

getting ads from that store. I have had friends tell me that merely mentioning a product when chatting through messenger triggered ads about it. We opt in by using this stuff.

Respondent 5: What's creepier is an email that popped up literally a day after I was talking to a friend on the topic (within earshot of my phone) and a picture I was describing popped up on Facebook.

Does any of this surprise you? It happens to all of us.

I'll bet that if Ronnie did an internet search for mattresses, she would probably get pages and pages of results and would encounter lots of banners and pop-up ads. She may have also found white papers and free guides and videos about mattresses and how to find the right one to suit her needs. Additionally, she might suddenly see ads for mattresses following her around the internet and on social media, and she might start receiving email marketing about mattresses.

All this information might help her make an

educated purchase, but there's a problem: it's information overload, and a bit invasive. How annoying! Does Ronnie really want to spend time sifting through all that information? No, she just wants to buy a mattress! If she spent the time required to read all of the available information about mattresses, she'd need to buy one fast because she'd be exhausted.

This example shows that the internet and your inbox have gotten overly crowded with marketing, creating confusion, which leads to doubt and skepticism. Exactly what we as consumers and marketers (like you) don't want.

When it comes to marketing, whether it's traditional marketing or digital marketing, as consumers, we pretty much hate it. It interrupts our lives and we want less of it. The amount of marketing we're exposed to is overwhelming and, at times, invasive. Many of us often try to avoid marketing altogether. Don't you agree? In fact, according to the 2017 PPAI Consumer Study,[1] we have become numb to most marketing:

---

[1] Promotional Products Association International, "Mapping Out the Modern Consumer: 2017 PPAI Consumer Study" (PPAI Research, 2016), 13.

- 68% of us don't watch online video ads
- 66% of us don't watch TV commercials
- 57% of us ignore digital ads
- 50% of us discard direct mail
- 48% of us ignore print ads
- 46% of us delete email marketing
- 46% of us don't listen to radio commercials
- 38% avoid mobile messaging
- 20% are not receptive to promotional products

If you take a hard look at those percentages and think about the implications, marketers are wasting a lot of money just trying to reach consumers to get their attention and influence them. For example, $68 of every $100 spent on online video ads is wasted, $66 out of every $100 is blown on TV ads, and $57 out of every $100 is flushed down the toilet with digital ads. Nearly half of all the money spent on direct mail, print ads (magazines, newspapers, etc.), email marketing, radio ads, and mobile messaging is thrown out the window. When it comes to marketing mediums, promotional products deliver the best bang for the buck because 80 percent of those surveyed are receptive to them.

I'm sure you'll agree that attracting new customers is no easy or inexpensive task, but it has to be done if a business is to grow. Do you recall the old saying "you can lead a horse to water but you can't make him drink"? Believe it or not, this concept applies to growing your business. It's a well-known fact that it can cost you up to six times more to attract a new customer than it costs you to continue a relationship with an existing customer. If you think about it, here's what you have to do to start a relationship with a new customer: first, you have to target the right people, then you have to promote your offering in a way that resonates with that market, then you have to catch them at their time of need, then you have to entice them to contact you, then you have to make sure they're a qualified prospect, then you have to put forth all the effort to convince the prospect to become a client, and then hopefully they buy. That's a lot of work! Maybe this is the reason we are inundated by advertising. When using these mass marketing mediums, marketers must spend incredible amounts of money just to get our attention because they know we consistently tune out a large percentage of advertising. What a huge waste of money!

Here's a perfect example of wasted marketing

money: One Saturday morning, I logged on to Facebook and saw a post by my friend Sara regarding Facebook ads. Here it is word for word:

> I am getting so frustrated with all these ads on Facebook. There seems to be at least one ad for every 3 posts...at least. Is there a way to turn off all the ads or do I have to attempt to do that with each one?

When I asked her if I could use her quote in my book, she agreed, and then she said:

> Add in my discontent. Those ads do not influence my buying habits at all, in fact because I am frustrated, I probably would not buy from them because of it! Just my two cents.

If you're spending money on Facebook ads, how would this make you feel? This is exactly what marketers DO NOT want to hear. Don't you agree?

Experienced marketers know at least some of their marketing money is wasted, but why do they keep spending dollar after wasted dollar? This question can be answered with one word: hope. Marketers hope their message eventually gets through and influences prospects and customers. The target market needs to be exposed to a marketing message many, many times before they take action, and the marketer is hoping the prospect or customer thinks of them the next time they need to make a purchase. Adding insult to injury, an individual prospect may never take action for the simple reason that they may never need the advertised product or service, which wastes even more marketing money. How sad.

If you want to get a better return from your marketing money, you need your customers and prospects to be exposed to your marketing message as much as possible at the lowest cost possible without annoying them. This way you can afford to keep your brand in front of them longer so they may think of you if and when the need arises. Naturally, this top-of-mind brand awareness can give you an advantage over your competitors.

There is a marketing medium most people actually like, keep, and use every day. It is welcomed into people's lives instead of avoided. This marketing medium is incredibly efficient at delivering a marketing message because it has the ability to cut through the disruption and noise caused by other marketing mediums. It creates a firm and lasting connection between an individual and a brand. I am, of course, referring to promotional products.

If you put your hand in your pocket, your purse, or your desk drawer, would you find a newspaper ad, a radio ad, or a billboard? How about a website? Do you have one of them hanging on your fridge? No, of course not. You may, however, have a pen in your pocket, a nail file in your purse, or a letter opener in your drawer. You may have a refrigerator magnet stuck to your fridge—and all of these items may be branded with a business's marketing message. These items are promotional products.

Promotional products are a $24+ billion industry, and they should no longer be looked down upon by marketers.[2] In my opinion, they might just be the best-kept secret in marketing. Smart marketers have learned that promotional products can target just about any demographic while staying within any budget, no matter how small. Do you want to target folks in rural Alaska? No problem,

---

[2] Promotional Products Association International, "2018 Sales Volume Study: Report" (PPAI Research, May 2019), 4.

send them imprinted ice scrapers. Promotional products are cost efficient, too. Once that marketer sends those ice scrapers to the folks in rural Alaska, the products will continue to deliver the marketing message over and over without interruption and without any additional cost to the marketer. Talk about targeted and low-cost marketing!

I often say promotional products are both a laser beam and a Swiss Army knife. With nearly eight hundred thousand products available, you can choose the perfect product to communicate directly with your target demographic. Do you think ice scrapers are an appropriate promotional product for those folks in Alaska? Would they be useful in Alaska? Of course! Can you imagine how cost-inefficient it would be to run ads in traditional media to get business from such a small and narrow market such as those folks in rural Alaska?

What are promotional products exactly? They're any product that is decorated with a marketing message that can be distributed to a customer, prospect, or employee. A promotional product is tangible advertising. Unlike newspaper, radio, TV, digital advertising, and other advertising mediums, promotional products are physical marketing, which creates interaction between the marketer and the target market. Promotional products incorporate all five senses: you can touch and see them, sometimes you can hear them, and yes, sometimes you can taste and smell them. An argument can be made that promotional products appeal to the emotional senses as well, such as a sense of belonging and sense of ownership.

People can get emotionally attached to a specific promotional product (or products). Over the years, I've had many customers refer to the items they buy from me as their "favorite bag" or "favorite pen." At times, I've heard them use the word "love" when referring to the items they purchase from me. They'll say things like, "I love this bag," or "I love these lip balms," or "My customers love the pens." Think about it—people also *love* to get free stuff, and if they love getting free stuff they love, doesn't this make promotional products a powerful marketing tool? You bet! I can't tell you how many reorders I get for bags, pens, calendars, chip clips, and so many other items because my customers tell me their customers *love* receiving the items. Do you think the recipients find the items they receive to be bothersome, invasive, or annoying? No way! The recipients welcome the items and use them.

Has a friend ever done something nice for you and you felt compelled to return the favor? Of course! If you didn't, you'd probably feel like a mooch, right? That's because there's a social norm called the Law of Reciprocity, which states that if someone does something nice for you, you will have a strong desire to do something nice for them in return. Sometimes, that strong desire encourages you to reciprocate by being even more generous when you eventually return the favor.

Distributing promotional products to customers and prospects taps into this hardwired human behavior. How many times have you said thank you to someone who gave you a promotional product? When you received that item, did you feel like you should somehow return the favor? Did you feel like you should do something nice for the giver, like allowing them a few moments of your time or an opportunity to earn your business, or at the very least, think kindly of them? Do other advertising mediums create this type of emotion? Hardly. While other marketing mediums may evoke some emotion, promotional products do that *and* build relationships and goodwill between consumers and a brand.

Promotional products are everywhere. It's

nearly impossible to avoid them, as they are woven into our daily lives. In fact, according to a survey I conducted during the summer of 2018, there's a 90 percent chance you have a promotional product in your possession right now. Another study done by PPAI found that 65 percent of consumers are exposed to promotional products at least six to ten times daily, and Millennials are in contact with promotional products at all times. When asked to rate which advertising vehicle encourages consumers to take action, promotional products were rated the most effective among Millennials, Gen Xers, Baby Boomers, and the Silent Generation.[3]

WHO IS PPAI?

The full name of PPAI is Promotional Products Association International, and it's a not-for-profit trade association for the promotional products industry. As a member of PPAI, my company receives products and services from PPAI that help us bring value to our customers. One of the many products and services we receive as a member are reports and surveys about how consumers use and interact with promotional products.

---

[3] 2017 PPAI Consumer Study, 6.

Do you want to reach people at their place of work? No problem, promotional products are a great way to do that. According to my Summer 2018 survey, 98 percent of those who responded claimed to have at least one promotional product in their workspace. Do you keep a radio ad at your desk? No, of course not, but you may have an imprinted coffee mug sitting on your desk. Do you want to reach people in their kitchen? Again, promotional products are a winner. My survey found that 95 percent of respondents have at least one promotional product in their kitchen. Do you still get the Yellow Pages? I still get them, and I used to keep them in a kitchen drawer. In the past, I used them with regularity, but now that book goes right into the recycling bin. I do, however, have an assortment of magnets, clips, pens, and other promotional products in my kitchen that get used every day. Maybe you do too. By the way, since most people work and most people have a kitchen, don't you think reaching prospects and customers in those places makes good sense?

I have a customer who's a big believer in promotional products and refers to them as "time-released marketing." He consistently buys and distributes them because he knows his marketing message will be seen by his prospects and customers over a long period of time. Sometimes the items are passed on to another person, which extends the reach of his marketing message a countless number of times. The 2017 PPAI Consumer Study found that 89 percent of the respondents recall receiving at least one promotional product within the past six months.[4] Eighty-one percent of them keep promotional products for more than a year because they are functional, fun, or trendy. According to the same study, 80 percent of consumers pass along a promotional product to another person if they don't keep it for themselves.[5] When given options to aid in recall, nearly nine in ten recipients are able to remember the branding, eight in ten can recall the messaging from at least one promotional product they received, and seven in ten remember the call to action.[6] Approximately 80 percent of recipients admitted to looking up the advertiser after receiving a promotional product. Eighty-two percent of recipients claimed to have a positive impression of the brand after receiving a

---

[4] 2017 PPAI Consumer Study, 14.

[5] 2017 PPAI Consumer Study, 6.

[6] 2017 PPAI Consumer Study, 7.

promotional product, and 83 percent are more likely to do business with the advertiser over other brands from whom they have not received a promotional product.[7] These compelling results indicate that promotional products deliver a lower cost per impression, and they create a memorable and favorable image of the advertiser, which influences the recipient. How's that for an efficient use of marketing money!

When was the last time you used a radio ad? When was the last time you lost your billboard and someone else picked it up? Does anyone welcome more TV ads? When was the last time you sat in front of your TV and said, "I want to see more TV ads"? How about pop-up ads on your computer; do you want more of them? On the flip side, you could invest about two hundred dollars (or even less) on a box of pens and distribute them to your customers, who will welcome and use them. What's even better is that your marketing message will be seen repeatedly at no additional charge to you. Unlike advertising mediums like email marketing, radio, TV, etc., recipients of those pens can't unsubscribe, change the channel, click "skip ad,"

---

[7] 2017 PPAI Consumer Study, 10–11.

or mute the marketing message printed on those pens.

That's powerful marketing! Can other advertising mediums make these claims?

Personal case in point: Back in the 1970s, when I was kid, my friend Bob gave me a duffle bag imprinted with the logo of a well-known truck manufacturer (I can't mention the name due to copyright and trademark restrictions). Bob received several of these bags from his mom's boyfriend, and he gave one to me. For years, whenever I stayed overnight somewhere or went on a trip with my family, I used that bag. Over forty years later, I remember the bag, the marketing message, and who gave me the bag. In contrast, I'll bet you don't recall the advertiser of the last ad you saw on TV, or the last ad you heard on the radio, or the last banner ad you saw on your computer.

This chapter opens with Ron Popeil's famous statement "set it and forget it," which, in my opinion, accurately describes why promotional products are such a powerful medium. After you incorporate them into a marketing plan and distribute them to your intended market, the promotional products start their important work delivering your marketing message. They are welcomed, kept, and used by recipients and are sometimes passed along to others, which furthers their reach. Best of all, the marketing message they deliver is seen repeatedly without interruption, without further involvement by you, and without any additional cost to you. Can marketing be simpler and more cost effective than that?

CHAPTER 2

PICKING THE PERFECT PROMOTIONAL PRODUCT

It ain't rocket science.

—Emeril Lagasse

If you're like most folks, you would probably jump on the internet to do a search if you planned to purchase promotional products. You'll quickly learn there are many companies that sell them, and you may be overwhelmed by the number of items available. If you click on one of the websites and surf a bit, you may find some items that seemingly fit your needs. But how do you know the items you find are of good quality by simply looking at a photo on a website? How do you know they will be delivered on time? You assume your logo and ad copy will be printed correctly, but how can you know this for sure? How will you know the products are safe?

In order to answer these questions, the first place to start is to learn how the promotional products industry is organized. The industry is made up of two parties: the supplier (sometimes known as the "factory") and the distributor. There are also two parties outside of the industry: the buyer (also known as the "end user") and the recipient (the person who actually receives and uses the item). Supplier companies manufacture, produce, and decorate the items with the buyer's marketing message. According to PPAI, there are approximately 3,500 suppliers in the United States. The total number of unique promotional products manufactured by the suppliers is somewhere around eight hundred thousand items. The suppliers sell their products through promotional products distributors, who market and sell the products to buyers, who then distribute them to the recipients. It's estimated that there are thirty thousand promotional product distributors in the United

States.[8] These are the folks who will guide you in selecting the perfect item to meet your goals by sifting through those eight hundred thousand products. It is their job to know the ins and outs of the suppliers and their products, the product specifications, imprinting methods, and delivery capabilities, so that you receive your order on time, and when you open the box, you will like what you see and your recipients will enjoy and use the items you give them.

Your first step in purchasing the perfect promotional product should be finding a qualified distributor who has a deep knowledge of the promotional products industry, the suppliers, and the products. Additionally, it is essential that this person has a strong background in marketing. This person will become your promotional products and marketing counselor and will be a reliable part of your marketing team. Over time, your counselor will learn about your business, business philosophy, and marketplace so they can make meaningful marketing recommendations. They typically

---

[8] Frequently Asked Questions, s.v. "How Is the Promotional Products Industry Organized?" PPAI, https://ppai.org/associ ation/frequently-asked-questions/.

work on commission so you can get expert advice without putting out any money up front.

Many promotional products look great on a website, brochure, or catalog, but there are additional factors and potential pitfalls that affect the final outcome of your order. An experienced counselor is well aware of these factors and will guide you in finding an item that works within your budget and meets your goals, determine if your logo and ad copy will print accurately, and make sure the order is delivered on time. Selecting the right promotional products counselor will dramatically reduce the time it takes to find the perfect item and will ensure you will love the final result.

In addition to being your promotional products and marketing expert, your counselor plays other important roles in the relationship. First, your counselor has an intimate knowledge of the items, production processes, and imprinting methods. They prepare your order and artwork in such a way that it accurately communicates the order's specifications with the supplier. This reduces the chance of your order being delayed due to supplier questions and production problems. Then, once the order is in the hands of the supplier, they shepherd your order through production to delivery. Lastly, in the event there is an issue, your counselor is your advocate and intermediary between you and the supplier, and they are experts at fixing any issues that pop up. Problems with orders can happen with regularity, and your counselor will often correct them without you even knowing they occurred.

A few words of caution:

The barriers to entry into selling promotional products are very low and turnover is high, so insist on working with an experienced counselor. There are many folks who get into the industry on a part-time or temporary basis. Also, there are many graphic designers, sign makers, and printers who sell promotional products as an additional service to their regular business. They often don't have the time or interest to learn as much as they can about the products, imprinting methods, and suppliers. While these folks may have some experience in the promotional products industry, they typically do not possess the knowledge base, research tools, resources, and supplier relationships that an experienced counselor acquires over years of practice. Seek someone who has years of experience and who sells promotional products as their full-time career.

A small handful of suppliers are willing to work

directly with buyers, and you may be tempted to circumnavigate the counselor. While this appears to be a way to save money, this is a bad idea. There are many components that go into producing a successful order, many of which you, as a buyer, may have little or no experience handling. If you choose to work directly with the supplier and something goes wrong, you are on your own. Good luck to you.

Whether you choose to work with a promotional products counselor or not, there are additional criteria you need to consider in order to make the perfect choice when purchasing promotional products:

1. **The most important criteria you need to consider is the marketing goal you'd like to achieve using promotional products and how the items will integrate into your overall marketing plan.** Without a clearly defined goal, you'll wind up distributing thoughtlessly chosen items to random recipients. This will result in a huge waste of money. Your goal will become the basis of your promotional products marketing plan, and from that, you will determine your

objectives to achieve that goal. When you create a realistic marketing goal, you'll make more efficient and effective choices selecting the items you buy, the messaging on the items, and the distribution method to get those items in the hands of your target market. This may sound a bit intimidating, but your counselor can help you. Also, your goal, plan, and objectives can be as simple or complex as you want. That's one of the benefits of marketing your business with promotional products. Below are some helpful questions to start you on your path to goal setting. Perhaps there are other questions that may be more applicable to your business, but here's a start:

- What are you trying to accomplish?
- Are you looking for more business from existing customers or new business from new customers?
- Do you want to thank your customers for working with you?
- Do you simply want your customers to have your contact info handy in case they need you?

- What do you want recipients to do when they receive your items? Do you want them to call you?
- Are you trying to incentivize your customers to refer you to others?
- Do you want to attract people to your trade show booth, come to your office, download your eBook, or watch a video?
- What outcome do you expect from your marketing? Is it realistic?
- How will you track your progress?
- How will you know you're reaching your objectives?

2. **Another obvious criterion to consider is finding products that appeal to your intended target market.** Note I say "intended target market." Promotional products often get passed on to others. I'm certainly not suggesting to exclude other groups, but focusing your marketing dollars on a group that is most likely to buy will put more money in your bank account. The more you know about your ideal prospects and customers, the more likely the products you choose will be enjoyed

by them and kept in their proximity. In a perfect situation, your promotional products will meld into the lives of your target market. This helps your marketing message penetrate and influence them to choose you when they are ready to buy.

Naturally, you'll need to be able to describe this group. Perhaps these questions can help you choose an appropriate item that appeals to your target market:

- Is your target market men, women, or both?
- Are they younger, older, or both?
- When do they buy from you, and what circumstances typically trigger a purchase?
- What problems do they have?
- What unique characteristics do they have?
- Do they have anything in common, and what are their differences?
- When they buy from you, who influences their purchasing decisions: their kids, their spouse, their employers or employees?

- Where are they when they make their decisions to buy from you? In their house? In their office? In their car? Sitting on the beach?
- Where do they work?
- Where do they play?
- What are their hobbies?

HELPFUL ADVICE:

If you take a look at your customer base, your prospects, or your niche market, you may need to purchase a number of different products that appeal to the different groups within your target market. For example, your customers may be both men and women. Purchasing products for each gender may result in a bigger impact.

Make sure the product you purchase is something your target market will enjoy and keep using over and over, even if it's a product you don't personally like. I'll restate for emphasis:

buy products your target market likes even if you don't like the actual product.

Don't make the product selection process complicated. The ideal product may be as simple as a pen or a magnet. If the perfect item that effectively carries the message to your target market is rudimentary, don't waste time searching for something more sophisticated.

Avoid custom-made products by any means necessary. When ordering custom, be prepared to shell out a lot of cash, because custom products are almost always much more expensive than off the shelf. Also, there is a higher chance something could go wrong with production, which may result in final product you don't like or a delay in the delivery.

If you plan to distribute an industry-related product to a specific industry market, make sure that product is top notch. For example, if you market to contractors and you want to distribute screwdrivers, make sure that screwdriver is high quality, otherwise you run risk of damaging your brand's reputation. The contractors know quality tools and will appreciate a good screwdriver. The high-quality screwdriver will enhance your brand by giving those contractors the impression you understand and care about their business. A low-quality screwdriver will hurt your brand. It's that simple.

Consider the message the products you distribute sends to your target market about your company. Buy items that best match your company values. What message do you hope recipients receive about who you are and what your company is all about? For example, if you distribute products made in the USA, you're messaging to your target market that you're supporting our country and American workers. Don't miss the opportunity to let your product selection tell a story about your business.

Lastly, if you're distributing the items at a trade show that attendees have to travel by plane to attend, make sure your items are TSA approved, otherwise your marketing money will be left at airport security when the attendees go home.

3. **Understanding the order timeline is important.** Do you have a deadline or are you using the items at an event? If so, the perfect

promotional product does you no good if it can't be delivered on time. You and your counselor will need to factor in time for product research and quoting (which can take hours or days), artwork creation and proofing (this too can take hours or days), order processing, production time, and transit time to your location. Production time and transit time are measured in business days when ordering promotional products. Weekends and holidays don't count because most suppliers are closed on those days and the shipping carriers don't deliver without steep fees. Also, your counselor's office may be across town, but your order might be shipping from the other side of the country, and that adds to the transit time.

The date you use the items is called your "use date" or "event date." Obviously, you will need the items delivered to you prior to that date. This date is known as the "in-hands date." If you have an event, let your counselor know the in-hands date and the event date immediately to ensure timely delivery. Be honest when you give your counselor the in-hands date. If you don't have an in-hands date, don't make one up for the sake of having the items arrive sooner. This may have unintended consequences. A made-up or inaccurate in-hands date may unnecessarily require the order to become a rush order. By doing this, you run the risk of having to pay additional fees and/or the chances of your order not being filled accurately increase. Also, asking your counselor to jump through hoops unnecessarily is unfair. It's best not to cry wolf when it comes to the in-hands date.

Here's a simple example of an order timeline. Let's say you're in Philadelphia and you have an event coming up. You discuss this event with your counselor, who does some quick research and immediately finds the perfect product, which happens to be manufactured in California. Let's say the production time on the product is seven days. Additionally, you don't have vector art (you'll learn about that later in chapter 3), so the art needs to be created, and that will add an additional day. Now you're up to eight days. Transit time from California to Philadelphia is four to five days. Now you're up to twelve to thirteen days—working days, that is. If you placed the order on a Monday morning, at the earliest, you will receive your order three Tuesdays later! And this is assuming you approve the proof in a timely fashion (production stops awaiting your proof approval), the supplier has inventory of the item, nothing goes wrong with production, or the shipping carrier doesn't lose or delay your order. Mother Nature can delay your order too. All these issues do occur and are real possibilities. I actually had an order that shipped from Minnesota to Florida that was delayed by a snowstorm in Ohio. Also, the suppliers ship many, many orders each day, and it's not uncommon that the supplier accidentally ships you someone else's order. If you planned ahead and nothing went wrong and your in-hands date is after that Tuesday, you're in great shape; if not, you might want to look into another product manufactured by a supplier who is closer to you or has faster production, or both. Stuff happens, so give yourself enough time to have the order arrive on time even if issues pop up.

One option to get your order delivered on time is to do a rush order. Many suppliers offer rush services. Some do it for free, some charge for it, but there are usually criteria that need to be met in order to qualify for rush service. Also, your counselor has to be available to process the rush order. If your counselor is in a meeting all day or out of the office or helping other customers, they won't be available to do any research, send you pricing, do the artwork, and process your rush order (or any order, for that matter). Rush orders typically put an added stress on production, and the chances of a mistake increase. If you have no choice but to do a rush order, pull the trigger as quickly as possible, because time is not on your side. Also, have a second and third product choice in case there is no inventory of the desired item, a machine breaks down, or Mother Nature interferes in some way. Obviously, the best course of action is to avoid rush orders if possible.

Another factor to consider when doing

an event is that you have to bring the items to your trade show booth and store them there. This isn't much of a problem if you purchase small items like pens, which are packed in smaller boxes with many pens in each box. Other items like mugs are larger and are packed in larger boxes with fewer items to a box. The smaller boxes are often lighter, easier to carry, and take up less space in your booth. The larger boxes are harder to manage and can take up a lot of space. I have a customer who gives out water bottles every year at a summer event. He keeps a supply of them at his booth, but when he runs out of them, he or someone helping him has to fetch more water bottles from his car. While the item is totally appropriate for his event, it's a drag that he has to do this.

4. **It's critical that you have a plan for distributing the products.** You could purchase the coolest, most cutting-edge product that is ideal for communicating to your target market, but if it never leaves your supply closet, you wasted your money. On the flip side, if

you have a distribution plan for the promotional products you purchased, any item, no matter how mundane, will do its job carrying your marketing message.

There are three basic distribution tactics for promotional products. I'll use a simple example to illustrate the distribution tactics. Let's say you purchased some imprinted pens. Here's how you can distribute them:

First, if you go to your mailbox today and find a bubble envelope, box, or mailing tube containing something inside, would you open it? Of course you would! When using direct mail, the key to success is getting your mailer opened, and lumpy mail almost always gets opened. You can mail or ship the pens to your target market in some packaging along with a sales letter and offer pitching a new item or service. This is the costliest distribution method, but it's quite effective. There's a very good chance your target market will actually see your marketing message and take action if your offer is enticing and the recipient is in the market to make a purchase. By the way, combining promotional products with other marketing mediums, in this case direct mail, increases your return on investment.

If you plan to mail promotional products, in this case a pen, it is critical to use the proper packaging and take some samples of your mailing to the post office for approval. By doing this ahead of your mailing, you will avoid costly mistakes, which include having your entire mailing wind up in the trash at the post office, having it returned to you, or having it delivered to your recipient postage due (very embarrassing). If you're doing a large mailing, I highly suggest finding a mail house in your area to handle your mailing. Any professional mail house will have a firm grasp on postal regulations and can offer options as to how to do your mailing most efficiently.

Second, you can actively hand out the pens. This tactic costs you nothing financially but does take a little bit of time and effort. For example, you could give those pens to restaurant servers when you go out to eat, you could give them to cashiers when you check out at a retail store, or you can give them out at an event. You could also purchase several items along with the pens and put them in a nice bag and give them to customers and prospects when they come to your place of business.

Third, you can simply leave the pens sitting out at your place of business or at a public place for people to take. For example, you could leave the pens in a cup on your desk so folks can take them as they come and go. The post office I frequent has a cup containing pens sitting on the counter. Perhaps yours does too, and you could put your pens in that cup. This tactic costs you nothing financially and requires little investment of your time and effort. The downside of this shotgun tactic is that it encourages recipients to take more items than they need and you get less control over who receives your marketing message. This increases the likelihood of wasted advertising money because your message may wind up in the hands of folks who are not your ideal customer. If you plan to use this tactic, I recommend purchasing small, inexpensive items in order to keep your costs down.

5. **Purchase quality products.** This is a no-brainer. As with any marketing medium, promotional products are an investment. The products you choose deliver much more than the marketing message; they represent you. Buy items that best match your company values and build your brand. A cheap pen that falls apart or an imprint that wears off after a short time makes you look bad and ultimately costs you more than the money you spent buying the items. What kind of message does distributing cheaply made products send to your target market? Well-made products last longer and communicate a positive message about you and your brand. Spend the money on quality, even if you have to buy fewer items.

In August 2001, I purchased pens for my business, and I actually have one of those old pens. The pen is almost eighteen years old as of this writing (June 2019). It's sentimental to me. I keep it in my desk drawer for safekeeping, so I don't see it very often. It writes just as good as it did the day I bought it. The current pricing on that pen is

$0.50 each, so the cost spread out over eighteen years is $0.028 per year.

I also have a chip clip from an order I sold in 1995. The funny thing is that the company advertising on that chip clip no longer exists. The chip clip lasted longer than the company! I keep and use the chip clip at work, and it still works perfectly and looks great. The clip has a magnet on the back, and when I'm not using it to seal a bag, the clip is stuck on my fridge. The current cost of that clip is $1.07 each, so the cost spread out over the last twenty-four years is $0.045 per year. That said, let's pretend I received that chip clip last year. I work at my office five days a week and I see it every time I go to my fridge, so I see it at least three times a day times five days a week. That's fifteen impressions per week. With time off and holidays, let's say I worked fifty weeks last year. That's seven hundred fifty impressions over the last year. The cost per impression over the last year is $0.0014 per impression. Talk about low-cost marketing!

I'm not saying all promotional products

will last as long as my pen and chip clip, but quality items will last longer than cheaply made items. Over the long run, the high-quality items will wind up costing you less.

Some key advice: When your order arrives, make sure you open all the boxes and inspect the entire order in a timely fashion. It might take a while to do this, but it's time well spent. This will give you the opportunity to make sure the items received are yours. This sounds obvious, but mis-shipments do happen and it's possible you may receive someone else's order. Also, production errors like incorrect item colors and imprint colors happen as well. Product and printing defects occur occasionally with all products, no matter how high the quality, so take the time to inspect for defects—especially anything with batteries, lights, or anything tech-related. Can you imagine how embarrassing it would be to give a good customer a USB drive only to find out from them it doesn't work? A few years ago, one of my calendar suppliers forgot to print the month of December in their calendars.

Fortunately, the error was caught early and corrected before my customers distributed them. It's best to find out there's a problem sooner rather than later, and putting in a claim right away will ensure it will be handled without much fanfare.

Lastly, if you're placing a large order and you're not familiar with the item, I highly suggest ordering a sample if you have time. Sometimes samples are free, sometimes you have to pay for shipping, and sometimes you have to pay for the item and shipping. Another option is to order a "spec sample." Most of the suppliers are willing to run a sample of the item printed with your artwork for a fee. This is a great way to ensure you will like the finished product, but in order to do this, you cannot be under time constraints and you will have to be willing to pay the fee.

6. **When crafting your marketing message, use a less-is-more approach.** The imprint area on promotional products is usually pretty small. You want recipients to see your marketing message, correct? Cluttering up the item with

lots of ad copy may require the use of small fonts, making your message difficult to read. Sometimes the imprint area is quite large, but resist the temptation to fill it up with lots of ad copy, as this could appear busy and distasteful. Imprinting your company name, phone number, or website should be adequate. Sometimes there's room to add an offer or catchy tagline.

If you have a logo, it can be added if there's room, and make sure you have a vector file of your logo with the Pantone® colors. The vector file is critical to your marketing success, and it is the file type most suppliers require. If you had your logo designed by a professional designer, they should have given you those files. If they didn't, give them a call and get those files, because they are valuable. You will most likely not be able to open the file, but that's okay. When you get the vector files, simply save them to your marketing folder and email them to your counselor when requested. Any qualified counselor will be able to open and use them. If you don't have a vector file, your counselor may be able to convert your logo to vector. You'll learn more about logos later in the book.

***

Now that you've learned how to make good promotional product purchasing decisions and how to avoid some pitfalls when ordering them, what products, out of the eight hundred thousand available, should you choose? Which items are the most popular, and which ones are most appropriate for your business?

Perhaps the PPAI 2018 Sales Volume Study[9] can help you in selecting a promotional product. This study ranks the most popular item categories by sales volume. Here they are:

1. **Wearables**
   a. *Apparel:* Uniforms, Shirts, Polos, Pants, Dresses, Activewear, Outerwear, Etc.
   b. *Fashion Accessories:* Footwear, Sunglasses, Aprons, Gloves, Vests, Robes,

---

[9] PPAI, "The 2018 Sales Volume Study: A Summary" (PPAI Research: 2019), http://static.ppai.org/public/research/industry%20sales/ppai2018salesvolumestudysummary.pdf.

Scarves, Baseball Caps, Flat Bill Caps, Helmets, Visors, Bandanas, Beanies, Headbands, Etc.

Does Not Include: Watches (Jewelry)

2. **Drinkware:** Water Bottles, Shaker Bottles, Vacuum Bottles, Flasks, Beverage Sleeves, Tumblers, Mugs, Thermoses, Stadium Cups, Pitchers, Decanters, Glassware, Etc.

Does Not Include: Bottle Openers (Kitchen), Coasters, (Kitchen), Bottled Water (Food and Beverage)

3. **Travel**
   a. *Bags:* Briefcases, Messenger Bags, Duffel Bags, Fanny Packs, Travel Bags, Laundry Bags, Totes, Backpacks, Etc.

   Does Not Include: Toiletry Cases (Travel Accessories), Coolers (Recreation), Pet Carriers (Pet), Gift Bags (Packaging)

   b. *Travel Accessories:* Passport Cases, Toiletry Cases, Luggage Tags, Garment Bags, Etc.

   Does Not Include: Wallets (Personal)

4. **Writing:** Pens, Pencils, Markers, Highlighters, Stylus Pens, Erasers, Etc.

5. **Technology:** USB Drives, Phone and Tablet Cases, PopSockets, Cell Phone Wallets, Phone Stands, Power Banks, Bluetooth Speakers, Headphones and Wireless Earbuds, Etc.

   Does Not Include: USB Car Chargers (Automotive), Stylus Pens (Writing)

6. **Awards:** Trophies, Plaques, Ribbons, Medals, Frames, Lapel Pins, Certificate and Diploma Folders, Etc.

   Does Not Include: Clocks (Date and Time)

7. **Office:** Folders and Binders, Notepads and Journals, Adhesive Pads, Stationery, Calculators, Rulers, Bookmarks, Clipboards, Letter Openers, Greeting Cards, Etc.

   Does Not Include: Planners (Date and Time), Certificate and Diploma Folders (Awards)

   Desk: Mouse Pads, Screen Cleaners, Business Card Holders, Paper Weights, Etc.
   Does Not Include: Staplers (Office), Desk Calendars (Date and Time), Stress Relievers (Games and Toys), Phone Stands (Technology)

   Health and Beauty

   a. *Medical and Safety:* First-Aid Kits, Pill

Boxes, Gel Packs, Bandage Dispensers, Etc.

b. *Hygiene and Grooming:* Hand and Body Lotions, Hand Sanitizers, Insect Repellents, Lip Balms, Soaps, Nail Files, Mirrors, Sunscreen, Toothbrushes, Floss, Wet Wipes, Etc.

8. **Event:** Balloons, Tents, Flags, Banners, Signage, Table Covers, Napkins, Lanyards, Badge Holders, Wristbands.
   Does Not Include: Name Badges (Buttons and Badges), Pennants (Spirit)
   Date and Time: Clocks, Wall Calendars, Magnetic Calendars, Planners, Etc.
   Does Not Include: Watches (Jewelry)

9. **Home**
   a. *Kitchen:* Appliances, Utensils, Placemats, Oven Mitts and Pot Holders, Cutting Boards, Measuring Devices, Coasters, Bottle Openers, Magnetic Clips, Etc.
   Does Not Include: Aprons (Fashion Accessories), Napkins (Event), Food Containers and Jars (Food and Beverage)

   b. *Tools & Decor:* Garden Tools, BBQ Grill Sets, Flashlights, Mats, Night Lights,

Candles, Fly Swatters, Ash Trays, Etc.
Does Not Include: Frames (Awards)

10. **Recreation:** Folding Chairs, Stadium Seat Cushions, Hand-Held Fans, Blankets, Lanterns, Umbrellas, Coolers, Yoga Mats, Exercise Bands, Beach and Sports Balls, Golf Accessories, Etc.
Does Not Include: Fit Bands (Jewelry), Rally Towels (Spirit)

11. **Personal:** Key Chains, Pocket Knives, Lighters, Money Clips, Wallets, Etc.
Does Not Include: Lanyards (Event), Cell Phone Wallets (Technology)
Labels: Window Clings, Stickers, Decals, Bumper Stickers, Temporary Tattoos, Shipping Labels, Etc.

12. **Automotive:** License Plate Frames, Air Fresheners, Window Shades, USB Car Chargers, Ice Scrapers, Etc.
Does Not Include: Bumper Stickers (Labels), Window Clings (Labels), Decals (Labels)
Games and Toys: Playing Cards, Stuffed Animals, Coloring Books, Puzzles, Stress Relievers and Spinners, Piggy Banks, Etc.

Does Not Include: Beach and Sports Balls (Recreation)

13. **Packaging:** Tissue Paper, Gift Bags and Boxes, Wrapping Paper, Etc.

Does Not Include: Ribbons (Awards), Shipping Labels (Labels)

Food and Beverage: Condiments and Spices, Candy and Mints, Bottled Waters, Gift Baskets and Tins, Food Containers and Jars, Etc.

14. **Buttons and Badges:** Embroidered Patches, Button Pins, Name Badges, Clothes Magnets, Etc.

Does Not Include: Lapel Pins (Awards), Badges (Event)

15. **Magnets:** Business Card Magnets, Mirror Magnets, Shaped Magnets, Etc.

Does Not Include: Magnetic Calendars (Date and Time), Magnetic Clips (Kitchen)

16. **Spirit:** Megaphones, Rally Towels, Pennants, Foam Fingers, Pom-Poms, Cowbells, Holiday Ornaments, Etc.

Does Not Include: Temporary Tattoos (Labels), Stadium Seat Cushions (Recreation)

17. **Jewelry:** Watches, Bracelets, Earrings, Dog Tags, Necklaces, Fit-Bands, Cufflinks, Etc. Does Not Include: Lapel Pins (Awards), Wristbands (Event), Flower Lei Necklaces (Spirit)
18. **Cards:** Gift Cards, Membership Cards, Loyalty Cards, Key Cards and Tags, Etc. Does Not Include: Greeting Cards (Office)
19. **Pet:** Pet Litter Scoops, Leashes, Collars, Pet Carriers, Etc.
20. **Other**

2018 SALES BY PRODUCT CATEGORY

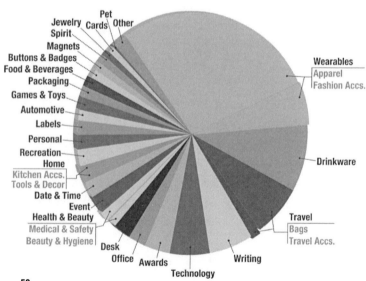

While some of these product categories may not necessarily be a good fit for your specific marketing goals, the study may indicate demand for specific product categories and can help you in selecting the right item to meet your objectives. That said, let's say key chains are a great way to market your business, but you see they are ranked eleventh on the list of sales volume. Does this indicate you should not use them to market your business, and that awards, which are ranked higher on the list, would be more effective for you? Of course not. Keep in mind that the study is based on sales volume and not units sold, so basing your buying decision on this measurement is just one option to consider. Keep in mind that many more key chains are sold each year in contrast to awards. Key chains are usually quite inexpensive, resulting in many, many more units sold, and the higher price tag of awards results in fewer units sold. If the study was based on units sold, the ranking of the item categories would be much different, because key chains would rank much higher.

Key chains and awards are completely different categories and are used by marketers for different reasons. If key chains are a better fit for you, then by all means use key chains, but you could still use awards, too. If you think creatively, you can use any product category to market your business. The following is a real-life example using lapel pins (which are in the awards category). After the tragic attacks on September 11, 2001, there was a strong sense of patriotism. About a month or so after that horrible day, one of my customers mailed out American flag lapel pins to her customers along with a short letter showing her support for our country. Nothing in the letter was about selling her products; in fact, the lapel pins were not printed with her logo. Her phone rang off the hook for weeks with customers thanking her for the pin, and this created selling opportunities for her.

One interesting thing to point out is that writing instruments is in the top five in terms of sales volume. Writing instruments are typically under two dollars per unit, with a large majority under one dollar. The items in the other top-five categories are usually at a significantly higher price point than the average pen, pencil, marker, or highlighter. This tells us there is a very, very high volume of units sold in the writing instrument category.

This sales volume study is just one indicator of popular items. Another option for choosing the perfect item is to consider that we are literally surrounded by promotional products. If you look around, you'll see them in every part of your life. You'll find promotional products in your car, bathroom, basement, garage, TV room, living room, bedroom, and even in your yard. Three of the most common places we keep them and use them regularly are on our person, in our kitchen, and in our workspace. If you were to purchase and distribute appropriate items to your target market that are kept and used in these three places, your marketing message would be seen repeatedly.

Many of the items found in these places have a wide appeal across all demographics, like the aforementioned pen and chip clip. But, if you want to focus on a specific demographic, there are products that would appeal to that group that would be kept and used in one of those three places. For example, if your target is teenagers, perhaps a smartphone item or backpack would work for you. If you need to get even more granular, you could offer nail files to teenage girls and printed footballs to teenage boys. Do you think those items might be found in the possession of those teenagers? Do you think they'll see the marketing message on those items over and over? YES!

In the summer of 2018, I conducted a survey to find out what promotional products people keep on their person, in their kitchen, and in their workspace. The survey was conducted using Survey Hero, and I distributed the survey to my friends on Facebook, LinkedIn, and Twitter. I also distributed the survey via email to my customers and friends. Some of them shared the survey via social media and email, increasing its reach. I blocked any person in the promotional products industry from taking the survey. The folks who took my survey came from all walks of life and from all over the United States. The respondents were a balanced mix of men and women ranging from their late teens into their seventies. Most folks were employed in various industries while some folks were retired, unemployed, homemakers, or students.

I received nearly 1,100 responses to each of the questions in the three-question survey. Not all respondents answered each question. Each question was multiple choice. The promotional products I chose for the answers to each question were picked based on the popularity of the items, my nearly thirty years' experience in the promotional products industry, and the likelihood that the item would be found in that location. The respondent had the option to select as many or as few of the choices that applied to them. The results of the survey provide solid evidence that if you distribute useful items that are kept or found and used in these three places, there's a really good chance that the recipient will be in regular contact with your promotional product and will be exposed to your marketing message. As mentioned previously, the promotional products industry has approximately eight hundred thousand items available in nearly two dozen product categories, so there are many, many products in addition to the items noted in my survey.

What follows are the survey questions, results, and some analysis:

Question 1: What kind of promotional products do you have on your body or in your possession at this moment? For example, do you have a promotional product in your pocket or purse? Are you wearing branded apparel?

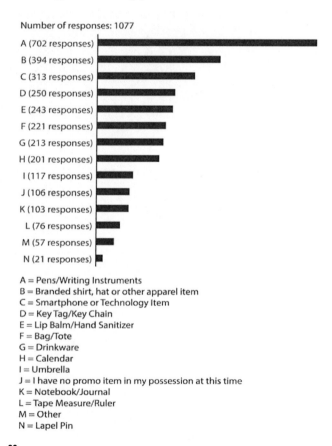

Number of responses: 1077

A (702 responses)
B (394 responses)
C (313 responses)
D (250 responses)
E (243 responses)
F (221 responses)
G (213 responses)
H (201 responses)
I (117 responses)
J (106 responses)
K (103 responses)
L (76 responses)
M (57 responses)
N (21 responses)

A = Pens/Writing Instruments
B = Branded shirt, hat or other apparel item
C = Smartphone or Technology Item
D = Key Tag/Key Chain
E = Lip Balm/Hand Sanitizer
F = Bag/Tote
G = Drinkware
H = Calendar
I = Umbrella
J = I have no promo item in my possession at this time
K = Notebook/Journal
L = Tape Measure/Ruler
M = Other
N = Lapel Pin

Question 2: What kind of promotional products do you have in your kitchen?

Number of responses: 1073

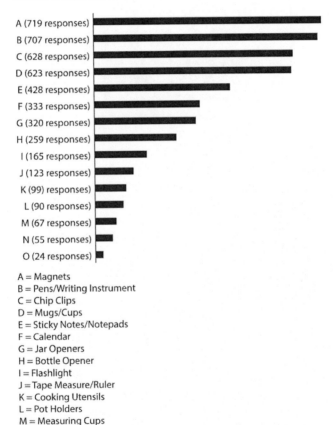

A = Magnets
B = Pens/Writing Instrument
C = Chip Clips
D = Mugs/Cups
E = Sticky Notes/Notepads
F = Calendar
G = Jar Openers
H = Bottle Opener
I = Flashlight
J = Tape Measure/Ruler
K = Cooking Utensils
L = Pot Holders
M = Measuring Cups
N = I have no promo items in my kitchen
O = Other

Question 3: What kind of promotional products do you have in your workspace? Skip this question if you do not have a workspace.

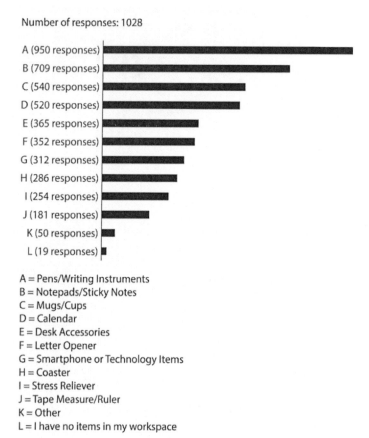

Number of responses: 1028

A = Pens/Writing Instruments
B = Notepads/Sticky Notes
C = Mugs/Cups
D = Calendar
E = Desk Accessories
F = Letter Opener
G = Smartphone or Technology Items
H = Coaster
I = Stress Reliever
J = Tape Measure/Ruler
K = Other
L = I have no items in my workspace

Takeaways Question 1: The result that sticks out the most is that only 106 out of the 1,077 survey respondents claimed to have no promotional products in their possession. This means that roughly 90 percent of the respondents had a promotional product on their person or in their possession at the time they took the survey. Nobody walks around with a billboard in their pocket, but they frequently walk around with a pen or lip balm in their pocket while wearing a shirt with a logo on it. Selecting any promotional product that is kept or worn on the recipient's person, whether it's mentioned in the survey or not, is smart marketing.

Thirty-seven percent of respondents claimed they were wearing branded apparel such as a shirt or hat at the time they took the survey. This is good news for marketers, because people like to wear apparel they find to be fun, cool, and enticing. It's virtually impossible to "unsee" a marketing message printed or embroidered on a garment. When worn by recipient, custom logo'd apparel becomes a walking billboard that works for the marketer without fail. Branded apparel has several functions: shirts, hats, sweaters, and jackets can be given to customers and prospects to promote a product, service, or event. Corporate apparel makes employees look more professional and builds credibility for your brand.

Nearly 29 percent of respondents claimed to have a branded smartphone or technology item in their possession. I'm sure you're not surprised, because our devices are so important to us these days. So, any item for use with a smartphone or tablet is effective marketing. Folks will keep and use these items because they find them functional. Lastly, 19 percent or more of the respondents had a calendar, drinkware, a bag or tote, lip balm or hand sanitizer, or a key chain or key tag in their possession when they took the survey.

Takeaways Question 2: Marketing your business using kitchen items is a solid winner because we spend a lot of time in our kitchen. We cook there, we eat there, and we congregate there. The kitchen is the hub of our homes. Fifty-five of the 1,073 people who took the survey claimed to have no promotional products in their kitchen. This means that 95 percent of respondents have at least one promotional product in the kitchen. When considering kitchen items, don't forget about pet-related items. People love their pets, and many of them eat and drink in the kitchen (mine does).

Not surprising, 67 percent of respondents have magnets, and roughly 58 percent have chip clips and imprinted mugs and cups in their kitchens. These items have long, useful lives, creating many impressions over the years. Nearly 40 percent of folks have sticky notes or notepads in the kitchen. The other items noted in the question, like jar openers, last long and come in handy in the kitchen, as do potholders, bottle openers, measuring cups, and cooking utensils. Tape measures and rulers have staying power. My parents have had the same yardstick hanging in the pantry for nearly fifty years. Lastly, flashlights are useful all over the house—most people need more than one of them.

Whether you're selling a product or service that's business-to-consumer (B2C) or business-to-business (B2B), you can bet that your kitchen-related promotional product will be seen and used regularly if it is useful or provides quick reference, or both. Here's an example. Let's say you sell B2B. You could distribute oven mitts with your marketing message to your target market. The oven mitts will be taken home and used by your target market. Now think about this: your branding is now in your target market's homes, and they'll see your message every time they use the item. Lastly, there are many kitchen items and other items that can be used around the home (garage, bedroom, basement, family room, etc.) that are not listed in the survey that could be a great fit for your business.

Takeaways Question 3: Only 19 people out of the 1,028 who took the survey reported that they have no promotional products in their workspace. This means roughly 98 percent of those who took the survey reported that there is at least one promotional product in the workspace. I'm sure you're not surprised to read that, as the workplace is loaded with promotional products. Keep in mind that the workspace is not always a traditional office. Many folks work from their cars, a home office, or places like coffee shops.

Pens are the most ubiquitous item in the workspace, with roughly 92 percent of respondents having at least one writing instrument (not a shocker). Sixty-nine percent had a sticky note or notepad. Approximately 50 percent had a calendar and a mug or cup. Over 28 percent had a coaster, smartphone or technology item, letter opener, or some type of desk accessory.

As with kitchen items, promotional products

for the workspace can reach your target market regardless of whether your product or service is B2B or B2C. We spend much of our time working, so any item that brightens our day or makes our job easier and more enjoyable is welcomed. Here's an example. Let's say you sell B2C. You could distribute lunch totes that your target market can use to take their lunch to work every day.

***

Pens (and writing instruments like pencils, highlighters, markers, etc.) were the most likely item to be found on the person of the respondent and in the workspace, and the second most common item found in the kitchen. Pens appeal to every demographic because everybody uses them. They are truly marketing workhorses, and folks will almost always be happy to receive another pen. Writing instruments like pens offer marketers a tremendous bang for their buck due to a pen's nature of getting lost or "stolen." They get shuffled from one person to the next, allowing the marketing message to be extended. They will filter through the community like tiny billboards. If you choose to add pens to your marketing plan, make sure you choose a quality pen. It will last longer, thus reducing your cost per impression.

The top four item categories found in the workspace (pens and writing instruments, notepads and sticky notes, mugs and cups, and calendars) are also products commonly found in the kitchen. This implies some of the products intended for home use may wind up at work (and vice versa). Mugs and cups sit out on people's desks at the office, so not only will the user see the marketing message, others will see it too. Travel mugs in particular may be used on daily commutes to and from work. Desk accessories and letter openers are items that are kept because they are useful, and they are good for marketing because they last a long time. Smartphone and technology items like screen cleaners and smartphone stands will see a lot of use, as will low-tech items like coasters.

Some of the items featured in the survey are inexpensive and consumable, like pens, lip balm, hand sanitizer, sticky notes and notepads, and calendars. Purchasing and distributing these items is a good option because they need to be replaced as they are consumed or misplaced. Some items are inexpensive and have longer useful lives, like magnets, chip clips, plastic stadium cups, jar openers, bottle openers, inexpensive flashlights, stress relievers, tape measures and rulers, letter openers, and key tags and key chains. Even if folks already have one of these items, they will often welcome another because they often need more than one.

Other items like apparel, bags and totes, mugs (tumbler, ceramic, etc.), smartphone and technology items, flashlights (higher end), cooking utensils, potholders, measuring cups, desk accessories, coasters, umbrellas, and notebooks and journals can be a bit more expensive. While the price tag on these types of items can be a bit higher, they have a higher perceived value, which increases the likelihood that the recipient will keep and use the item throughout its long life. This creates many impressions, which reinforces your marketing message on the user and others who are exposed to the item, and this reduces the cost of the advertising. Personal case in point: Back in 2005, one of my suppliers gave me an umbrella imprinted with their logo. I still use it, and it works perfectly.

A note about calendars: They are still relevant. Yes, people do use the calendars on their smartphones, but they are still using paper calendars, too. Calendars are often found hanging in the kitchen being used to coordinate family schedules. Wall and desk calendars are found in most workplace settings. Users find it much easier to glance at the calendar on their wall or desk than to de-task to check their smartphone or locate the calendar on their computer. The price of a promotional calendar can vary quite a bit, but most cost between one and three dollars per unit, making the cost per impression just pennies per day. My customers who see the most success marketing with calendars actively distribute them by mailing them or dropping them off at their customers' offices and other businesses. One of my customers takes them to the DMV near her office.

A final note about my Summer 2018 survey: I counted and tabulated every response. I received 1,077 responses for Question 1 (items found on your person) and discovered that the average person had 2.69 categories of promotional products on their person when they took the survey. I received 1,073 responses to Question 2 (items found in the kitchen), and the average person had 4.25 categories of promotional products in the kitchen. I received 1,028 responses to Question 3 (items found in the workspace), and the average person had 4.39 categories of promotional products in their work-space. Note that I say "categories of promotional products" and not number of promotional products.

This can be significant because the respondent may be in possession of or be in contact with more than one item in a specific category. For example, if a respondent claimed to have pens in her workspace, this could indicate that there is one promotional pen in her workspace (unlikely) or more than one promotional pen in her workspace (highly likely). The survey asked the respondent which product categories were found in specific locations, but did not ask the respondent to count the number of individual items within each product category.

I opened the chapter with a quote by Emeril Lagasse, so here's some food for thought—many times throughout my career, customers and prospects asked me which promotional products would be most successful for them or what promotional products work best in their industry. The shortest answer is all marketing works, but there is no marketing magic bullet. If there were, we'd all be rich and marketing would become irrelevant. John Wanamaker famously said, "Half the money I spend on advertising is wasted; the trouble is I don't know which half."

That said, after being in the promotional products industry for nearly thirty years, I am convinced that my customers who actively and consistently market their businesses place orders with me regularly. Some of them purchase items to be used in conjunction with a program to welcome new customers, to provide contact and reference information, or to generate leads. The items they buy are the items commonly found on our person, in our kitchen, and in our workspace. These folks have kept their marketing simple by choosing quality items they can efficiently distribute. They don't make changes to the items, the colors, and the ad copy for the sake of doing something different. This indicates to me that they are having some success with these items at some level. If they didn't, they wouldn't keep buying these items.

The key to using promotional products to market your business is to choose a quality product that is appropriate for your target market, having it imprinted with a clear, concise message or offer, and having a plan to distribute it. It's really that simple.

In keeping with the Emeril Lagasse theme, here's some dessert. I received many comments from those who participated in my survey. The most common theme of their comments centered around the revelation that the respondent didn't realize promotional products were a big, and often subtle, part of their life. After taking the survey, the respondent discovered that promotional products were integrated into their lives.

If you take a look at your life and your surroundings, how many promotional products do you find?

CHAPTER 3

DO YOU HAVE A PERFECT LOGO?

This is a football.

—Vince Lombardi

When you think of your business's assets, you'll probably think about property such as real estate, office furniture, and computers. You might also think of your customer list. But there's one business asset that often gets little attention: your logo. While this book is about promotional products, I think it's important to discuss logos because most promotional products are printed with a logo. You want your promotional products to look great when you receive your order, right? If you have a logo, hopefully it's what I call a "perfect logo." If you don't have a logo, you should consider having one designed.

I'd be willing to bet most people would say a great logo needs to be "creative" and "memorable." While these criteria are true, having a creative and memorable logo does not guarantee the logo will look great when it's reproduced on a promotional product or any other marketing collateral. If you think about it, the most important criteria of a logo is what it will look like after it's printed. A logo that does not print well is practically worthless, regardless of how beautiful it looks. A poorly designed logo is more of a liability than an asset. A well-designed, mechanically sound logo will print accurately, and this enhances your company's image and message. A perfect logo is critical to your marketing success.

Since I began my career in the promotional products industry in 1990, I've printed everything from business cards to whoopee cushions, and most of these items were imprinted with a logo. I've literally printed millions of items, and I've worked with thousands of logos—some of the logos printed well, while others did not. I've come to the conclusion that the logos that printed well have common characteristics. These logos rarely (if ever) gave me or my suppliers any trouble, and my customer was happy with the results when their order arrived. This is why I call them perfect logos.

THE PERFECT LOGO CHARACTERISTICS ARE:

1. Perfect logos work well in black and white. A perfect black-and-white logo will increase the options for how it can be reproduced. There are instances when you'll need to have the logo printed in black or a single color due to production or cost restrictions. I suggest having your logo designed in black and white first. Once you have a black-and-white logo that looks good to you, you can add color (or colors) later.

If you decide to incorporate color into your black-and-white logo, I highly recommend creating the logo in a maximum of two "spot" colors (i.e. two individual colors). Logos with more than two spot colors can be more expensive to print, and most suppliers can do two-color printing much more efficiently than printing in more than two colors. If your multiple-color logo is not designed in spot color, it will have to be reproduced via full-color printing, which really limits the logo's ability to be printed on a variety of items.

2. **Perfect logos are legible at just about any size.** This may seem like a simple idea, but I've seen logos that look great at one size but are almost indistinguishable when reduced by as little as 25 percent. Before settling on a design, make sure your logo looks clear and legible when it's reduced or enlarged.

3. **Perfect logos are created from solid colors and do not contain any shading, gradients, screens, or halftones.** For example, the logo should not have black that fades into gray. This effect may not be able to be printed on some items and can sometimes be more expensive to print on those items that can accommodate this effect.

4. **If a perfect logo has multiple colors, the colors do not touch one another.** If the registration (i.e. the alignment of the colors) is off when the item is printed, it will be very noticeable and look horrible. Also, a multiple-color logo with touching colors makes it difficult to reproduce the logo in one color when necessary because it becomes indistinguishable where one color stops and the other begins. If

the colors do touch, make sure one of the colors can be removed without ruining the integrity of the image. This is another reason it's imperative that you have the logo designed in black and white first.

5. **Perfect logos do not have fine details or tiny fonts.** These elements are difficult to reproduce accurately. Fine details and tiny fonts drop out and become difficult to see when the size of the logo is small.

6. **The owners of perfect logos have in their possession the native vector files, the Pantone® colors (a.k.a. PMS colors), and the names of the fonts used, and the fonts are outlined.** Perhaps what I just said is jargon to you, but it's important to understand that your logo is a construction of a number of parts. A professional designer understands and uses these parts to design your logo and should be able and willing to provide these files and information to you. If your designer doesn't know or understand these terms and cannot (or will not) provide them to you, find a new designer.

Have you ever enlarged a .JPEG file and it looked jagged and fuzzy? The .JPEG file, and many other file types, are known as "raster files," and they are not as useful as vector files. They cannot be scaled larger without becoming distorted, they cannot be altered in any way, and they cannot tell your designer, printer, or promotional products counselor the colors in your logo. Vector files are used to print just about anything, and they will produce the highest-quality imprint. Your promotional products counselor will ask you for one when you order. If constructed properly, vector files can be scaled larger without distorting visually like the .JPEG, and they can provide your counselor with the correct colors in your logo. They can also be altered if necessary. The extensions for the vector files are .AI (Adobe Illustrator), .EPS (encapsulated postscript), and they also can be .PDF depending on how your designer saves the original vector file. When you receive these files from your designer, you most likely will not be able to open them. Don't delete them because you can't open them! The files require design software to open and manipulate them and most people don't have this software. Any counselor worth their salt will have this software and will be able to provide a proof to you. Remember, your logo is an asset. Simply save the vector files to a drive and email them to your counselor when requested.

One last bit about file types: common file types such as .JPEG, .PNG, .TIF, .GIF, .PUB, .PSD, .BMP, .WMF, and Word files are *not* native vector files, and you cannot save one of these files as a vector file. If you "Save as" one of these files as an .AI or .EPS file, they don't become usable vector art. These files can, however, be converted to a vector file by a professional designer, but this is not always recommended because it's always best to work with the original, native vector file.

If you have a company logo and it meets these design requirements, it will work well on just about anything, from business cards to billboards. If it does not meet these guidelines, I recommend having it redesigned. If you don't have a logo and want to hire a designer to create a logo for you, please make sure you forward these guidelines to your designer.

SOME FINAL ADVICE ABOUT LOGOS:

1. **Hire an experienced designer who knows how to design for all marketing mediums.** Strong emphasis on "experienced." A web

developer may not design a logo that works well for print, and a designer who knows how to design for print may not design a logo that looks good on the internet. Also, your nephew in design school or your next-door neighbor's daughter may be able to design something that looks pretty, but my experience tells me that the chances of the logo meeting the perfect logo guidelines are slim. A qualified designer is invaluable and can make your company look like a big brand. Great design can do that.

2. **As you go about your day, pay attention to the logos of the big brands.** You'll notice they pretty much meet all of the characteristics I outline above. Big brands know the value of a perfect logo.

3. **If you can't afford to have a perfect logo designed or your business is newly formed, use a basic font for your company name.** Buying a logo on the cheap or too early may require you to make too many changes to it as your business evolves, and this creates mixed messages in the marketplace. It's best to wait until

you have the money to do it right and/or your business is more established. The old adage "measure twice, cut once" applies here.

Do not use clip art or images you find on the internet for your logo, because it will make your brand look unprofessional and make you look like an amateur. These clip art images are available to everyone, and someone else may already be using the same image, which can cause confusion among buyers. In fact, one of my customers in the Philadelphia area is using the same exact piece of clip art as one of my customers in the Chicago area. Also, the clip art files are rarely, if ever, available in vector format, so they'll have limited print capabilities. Lastly, some of these files have legal restrictions like copyrights and trademarks.

4. **If your logo incorporates an icon along with a font, make sure the icon and the font can be separated and used apart from each other.** There are circumstances when this becomes necessary. For example, the Golden Arches in McDonald's logo can be separated from the "McDonald's" font so that either design

element can be printed by itself. The Golden Arches icon is so powerful it can stand alone, and everyone knows what it means. There are instances when the Golden Arches and/or the word "McDonald's" looks better or is more effective all by itself.

5. **If you have a perfect logo, resist the urge to change it for the sake of "trying something new" or "freshening it up" with the hope that this will create a flood of new business.** The longer you keep your logo "as is," the more brand equity it will build for you over time. Changing your logo will most likely not bring you the results you expect, so leave it alone unless it needs to be fixed mechanically. As I've said to my customers many times, McDonald's never changes the Golden Arches.

I quote the great Green Bay Packers coach Vince Lombardi in the opening of this chapter. Coach Lombardi's famous phrase was part of a speech to his players prior to the 1961 season. His speech stressed the perfect execution of football fundamentals like blocking and tackling in order to be successful. This laser focus on the basics helped Vince Lombardi become one of the greatest coaches in sports history. From that season forward, he never lost in the playoffs, and he won five NFL championships over the next seven years.

A perfect logo is fundamental to your marketing success. It's the cornerstone of your marketing communications, and it is often the first point of contact between your company and your prospects and customers. Your logo works for your company endlessly without taking a break, twenty-four hours a day, seven days a week. A perfect logo will reproduce accurately on many promotional products, which will build your brand, and that will ultimately put more money in your bank account.

CHAPTER 4

43 EXAMPLES OF HOW OTHERS HAVE USED PROMOTIONAL PRODUCTS

Do. Or do not. There is no try.

—Yoda

Over the years, I've had many conversations with customers about promotional products, and they often center around helping them reach a marketing goal. Perhaps they want to keep their name in front of their customers to help increase customer retention, or get a referral from them. Maybe they want to create upselling and cross-selling opportunities to help them get more business from existing customers. Sometimes they want to generate leads by prospecting for new customers or attracting prospects to their trade show booth. Perhaps you have similar goals.

Whatever your marketing goals may be, promotional products can help you reach them by forming a bond between your company and your customer or prospect. In my opinion, one of marketing's most important roles is to create opportunities and start (or continue) conversations and relationships between buyers and sellers, which may eventually lead to a sale. Promotional products have a unique ability to connect buyers and sellers and keep them connected.

What follows are forty-three examples of how other marketers used promotional products to help them reach their goals. All of these clever ideas were successful because the item was a good fit with the marketer's target market, the marketer put forth the effort to distribute the items with strategic intention, and they did it consistently.

While I may mention a specific type of business in these examples, these creative ideas could work for just about any business—including yours. The fact is that while your business is unique, it's not much different than the next. Glean these examples for ways you can apply the concepts to your business. For example, an insurance agent and a landscaper are two distinctively different types of businesses, but they may have the same target market (for example, homeowners). So, an idea that works for an insurance agent might just work for a landscaper. Make sense?

1. Prospect for new business using imprinted flyswatters.

I have a customer in the insurance business who was looking for new customers and wanted to canvas a neighborhood near her office. She chose to do flyswatters imprinted with her contact information and the tagline "We Swat the Competition." She and her college-age daughter used a hole punch to create a hole in a company brochure. Then they threaded a string through the hole in the brochure, then through the hole in the flyswatter, and tied it off. On a nice spring day, she and her daughter went door to door and hung the flyswatters on the doorknobs of the homes in that neighborhood. Here's the brilliance of her idea: the recipient may not keep the brochure, but there's a good chance they'll keep the flyswatter, which features her name and contact info.

2. Open doors with bottle openers.

John O'Dea is a realtor in the New Jersey Shore town of Avalon, New Jersey. He wanted something to give out to renters when they booked with him and to folks who are buying or selling a home. John chose high-quality, long-lasting bottle openers. Since folks like to drink beverages at the shore, his customers and prospects will see his name and contact info every time they open their favorite beverage with his bottle opener. Additionally, when he meets new prospects, he often uses the bottle opener as a business card, and when he shows a home, he leaves the bottle opener on a countertop in lieu of the customary business card.

John O'Dea's Bottle Opener

3. Prospect for new customers using flying discs.

A few years ago, on a Saturday morning in April, I was walking my dog and I started noticing lime-green flying discs (the generic name for a Frisbee®) strewn on the lawns in my neighborhood. A landscaping company looking for new business in the area had them printed with their contact info, and then they drove through my neighborhood and threw them on my neighbors' lawns. They actually took an extra step in that they had waterproof labels imprinted with additional information, which they affixed to the underside of each flying disc. At some point during the day, my neighbors fetched the flying disc off the lawn and no doubt saw the marketing message. Perhaps they kept the flying disc, which delivered the landscaper's marketing message every time my neighbors saw the disc.

4. Attract people to your trade show booth using imprinted coloring books.

I have an insurance agent customer who has a clever way of getting his target market to come to his booth at community events in his town. As parents with small children walk past his booth, he offers the kids coloring books and cookies. Like a magnet, the offer is too strong for the kiddos to resist, so they drag their parents over to my customer's booth. My customer gives the kids their reward, which gives my customer the opportunity to engage with the adults. The coloring books are imprinted with his contact information, so when the family arrives home, the parents will be reminded of my customer.

5. Keep kids occupied at your office using imprinted coloring books.

Do customers ever bring their kids to your office? Sometimes they're a bit rambunctious, and this makes it a bit of a challenge to do business, right? Be prepared by purchasing coloring books to give out to the kiddos to keep them occupied and out of your hair while you're trying to work with Mom and Dad. The coloring books can be printed with your contact info so Mom and Dad will be reminded of you when they get home.

6. Say thank you and ask for referrals with reusable grocery totes.

One of the most popular items I sell are reusable grocery totes. I receive many reorders for them. They're durable, so they'll last for years. Many of my customers give a few to their customers as a thank-you gift after completing some business with them. As they give their customer the bags and thank them for their business, they'll tell the customer that if they need more bags, they can stop back to their office at any time. Additionally, they'll tell the customer that if one of their friends or a family member likes the bag or asks about it, they can stop by the office for a free one. This suggestion is a lead generator because it's a soft way of asking for a referral. Lastly, many of my customers make it a point to show the recipient that their contact info is printed on the bag in case they need them.

7. Attract people to your trade show booth with sturdy wooden backscratchers.

One of my insurance customers, GMI Insurance of Phoenixville, Pennsylvania, wanted something different to attract trade show attendees to their booth. They came up with a creative idea: give out quality wooden backscratchers. In the early 2000s, they contacted me with their request, and after some research I found a durable, well-made backscratcher. The item was heavy-duty, so it would be long lasting, and it had a large imprint area for my customer's message. GMI continues to order them because they are still a huge hit at trade shows. In fact, Karen Trudel, COO at GMI Insurance, told me that people swarm their booth to get a backscratcher. What a great way to attract sales opportunities! Lastly, I ordered a sample backscratcher from the very first run back in the early 2000s, and it sits on my desk every day and I use it regularly. I even wrote my name on it in case it "gets lost."

8., 9., 10. Branded beach balls bounce and bring more business.

One of my customers sponsored a summer concert series in his hometown, and he chose to purchase imprinted beach balls to carry his marketing message. He made arrangements with the promoter of the event so he could bring his beach balls to the concerts. He blew some of them up with a pump and then threw them out into the crowd. He told me the beach balls were bouncing around from person to person during each concert. Then, he handed out hundreds of them to the attendees as they left when the concert ended.

Another creative use for beach balls is to hand them out to kids when they come to your office with Mom and Dad. As the kids are tuckering themselves out by blowing up the beach balls, you can get some work done. When the family leaves your office, they'll take the beach balls with them and bring your contact info home.

Sue Traxler, owner of Traxler Insurance in Churubusco, Indiana, purchased beach balls to hand out at a town parade. She said they were a big hit, as people were seeking her out to get one. The beach balls were blown up by the parade attendees and seen bouncing all over town that day. As it turns out, the parade day was exceptionally hot, and the local newspaper did a story about folks cooling themselves off in the pool behind the firehouse. Naturally, Sue's beach balls found their way into the pool and into the news story. Since the beach balls were such a success, she purchased them the following year for the same event.

11. Show school spirit with cowbells.

Like many towns across our country, high school football is a passion to the people in the town of Ravenswood, West Virginia. Teresa Thacker of Ravenswood Insurance wanted to show her support for her team, so she ordered cowbells and handed them out at the homecoming parade before the big game. The cowbells were printed with her agency contact info on one side and the school mascot on the other. The cowbells scored big! By the time half the parade passed Teresa's office, word spread about the cowbells, and folks were calling her office asking her staff to a reserve one for them. Later that evening at the homecoming game, the cowbells were heard throughout the stands, making noise and showing school spirit. The cowbells will continue to score long after the game has ended; since they are a keepsake item, people will be reminded of the fun they had at the game every time they see the cowbell.

12. Corporate logo'd apparel creates opportunity.

Whenever you see someone wearing a shirt with a company logo on it, do you find yourself looking at it, even if it's just for a quick glance? When people wear logo'd apparel, they're wearing a little billboard, which creates thousands of impressions during its useful life.

One of my insurance customers happened to be wearing his logo'd polo shirt at the supermarket, and when he was going through the checkout line, the gentleman behind him struck up a conversation by asking my customer if he was in the insurance business. Of course, my customer replied yes. The man told him he owned a small apartment building in the area and was looking for a new insurance agent. He asked if my customer wrote that type of insurance and if he would be interested in quoting it. Naturally, my customer jumped at the opportunity. My customer quoted the insurance and eventually won the account . . . and it all started because he was in the supermarket wearing a shirt embroidered with his logo.

13. A doggone great T-shirt idea

When using T-shirts to market a business, the message and/or artwork needs to be attention grabbing. If the messaging is fun or unique, recipients will be encouraged to wear the T-shirts, and the messaging may start a conversation between the recipient and folks who see the T-shirt and its unique message.

Back in the day, I had a customer who was a pet sitter and dog walker, and she had one of the best T-shirt ideas I've ever seen. She ordered pink T-shirts that were printed in navy blue on both sides, and navy-blue T-shirts printed in white on both sides. The back of the T-shirts were printed with her contact info. The message on the front of the pink shirts was "Sit. Stay. Good boy." and the message on the front of the navy T-shirts was "Sit. Stay. Good girl." She gave the pink shirts to women and the navy shirts to men. She wore her T-shirts when she met with customers and cared for their pets, and she gave her shirts to her friends, family, and customers. Do you think the shirts created a reaction and started conversations?

14., 15., 16. Write more business with custom-printed notepads.

Custom-printed notepads are useful and inexpensive. Who doesn't need a notepad, right? Nick Yelovich at E. F. Butz Agency in Emmaus, Pennsylvania, has a clever and effective way to market the insurance agency with notepads. Whenever Nick needs to send correspondence to a customer, he writes the note on the top sheet of a notepad and then mails the entire notepad along with the other correspondence to his customer. The customer then receives the correspondence with Nick's note and gets to keep the notepad, which is printed with the agency contact info.

Another customer of mine bundles five custom-printed notepads together with a nice ribbon and then slides a pen under the ribbon. She uses the notepad/pen bundle as a leave-behind when she visits a customer or prospect or as a thank-you to customers who come to her office. Lastly, she makes sure the recipient knows her contact info is printed on the notepads. By the way, I have several customers who do something similar—they substitute pads of sticky notes for the notepads.

As a growth catalyst, Michael Gidlewski of Achievement Unlimited swears by custom-printed notepads. He orders a large, fifty-sheet 8.5x11 notepad printed with his contact info and something inspirational. He hands them out to attendees at his leadership workshops and mastermind groups and always makes sure his clients have a good supply of them at their workplace. The notepads are used for goal setting and brainstorming, and every time one of his clients, prospects, or workshop attendees uses a notepad, his logo and marketing message is reinforced.

Michael Gidlewski's Notepad

17. Combine stadium cups, beverage coolies, and pens.

I have a customer who sells a product to new car buyers and seeks referrals from car salespeople. Over the years, he has developed relationships with auto dealership owners and managers, and he came up with a brilliant idea to attract more referrals from the salespeople. He packs two beverage coolies and a bunch of pens into a sixteen-ounce stadium cup. He worked out an arrangement with some of the owners and managers that he could put those bundles on the desks of the dealership's salespeople. The items eventually disappear from the salespeople's desks into the hands of their customers and prospects. He visits the dealerships to replace the bundles, giving him the opportunity to network and interact with the dealership salespeople.

18. Pie plates are not pie in the sky.

A realtor in the Pittsburgh area gives her customers ceramic pie plates with her contact information glazed onto the plate as a thank-you gift to her clients. While not everyone bakes pies, the pie plates can be used to bake other yummy dishes, like nachos. Since the pie plates are high quality and long lasting, every time one of her clients uses the plate, they'll see her name and contact info.

19. Write more business by marketing with pens.

In the early 2000s, I offered marketing consulting as an add-on service to my customers. I did not actively market the consulting, as it was not part of my core business, but it was quite lucrative. I was paid a $3,000 retainer in addition to billing my customers for the promotional products and marketing collateral.

After some deliberation, I eventually decided to put some effort into marketing the service, and I came up with an idea that paid off handsomely. The marketing piece included a pen, a note, and a mailing tube. The pen was custom printed with my logo, phone number, and the tagline "Marketing Services for Hire." The note was printed with a brief message pitching my consulting services and my contact information. The note was a custom size that was folded and slipped beneath the clip on the pen. The pen/note marketing piece was inserted into a mailing tube, and then the tube was sealed. I had them bulk-mailed to approximately five hundred companies in my area. In terms of bulk mailing, this is a fairly small mailing.

Over the next few weeks or so, I received approximately a few dozen calls as a result of the mailing. The $3,000 retainer scared off all but one prospect. My mailer opened that door for me, and I wound up selling that prospect on my consulting services.

I worked with them for only about a year until their incumbent service provider got wise to me interloping and started to pay better attention to the customer. During the time I worked with the customer, I sold them over $20,000 in promotional products and printing in addition to the $3,000 retainer. The mailing cost me about $1,000, so I think I got a good return on my investment.

Avery Manko's Pen and Note Mailer

20. Donuts for dollars

Kristine Eilers of Comaltex Insurance Agency of New Braunfels, Texas, has a simple yet brilliant idea to encourage referrals from realtors and mortgage brokers. She purchases custom-printed donut boxes and fills them with donuts. The sales reps then stop by real estate and mortgage offices to drop off the tasty treats. The boxes have business card slits for a business card, and they communicate the agency contact information and lines of insurance they write. The marketing message is seen every time someone reaches into the box to get one of those delicious donuts. Additionally, the boxes are dropped off at their commercial clients, along with information about the personal lines insurance products.

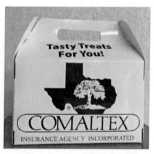

Comaltex Insurance Agency's Donut Box

21. Grocery totes, 50 percent off

One of my insurance customers has a family member who owns a restaurant that has a brisk carry-out business. Together, they came up with an idea to split the cost of ordering the reusable grocery totes. Their plan was simple: my insurance customer had her marketing message printed on one side of the bag, and the restaurant had their restaurant logo and contact information printed on the other side. My insurance customer kept half the bags at her office and distributed them to her customers. The other half of the bags were kept at the restaurant and were used for the carry-out business. Not only did both businesses save money on the actual advertising, but most importantly, they helped cross-promote each other's business.

22. Magnetic sports schedules are a winner.

Realtor Tim McGoldrick of Chestnut Hill, Pennsylvania, sends his customers magnetic sports schedules. The schedules are made from a card stock that has a magnet at the top. The magnet has a strip that peels away, allowing Tim to affix his business card, which includes his photo. In early August of each year, he sends his customers the Philadelphia Eagles football schedule, and in early March, he sends them the Philadelphia Phillies schedule, which allows Tim to share his marketing message for nearly a full year. When he sends the schedules, he includes a flyer of some of his current listings. The schedule and flyer are fairly inexpensive, and with postage, the whole mailer costs less than a dollar. Tim has been distributing these schedules for years, and his customers have come to expect them. Some even contact him prior to each season to make sure he sends them a schedule. Additionally, Tim has made arrangements with several retail businesses in his area to allow him to leave a pile of the schedules on their counters so their customers can take them. Any leftover schedules are kept as giveaways for when he meets new prospects. He also leaves them on the refrigerator of any homes he shows to a buyer. As a final note, in speaking with Tim about this case study, he shared with me that he was once eating in a restaurant and was approached by a man who said Tim looked familiar. After some small talk, they couldn't find the connection and the man walked away. Moments later, the man came back and told Tim he realized his face looked familiar because he had one of his Phillies schedules on his refrigerator.

23. A clever slogan on beverage can coolies creates a stir.

Insurance agent Josh Bagby of Canton, Georgia, ordered a very popular product: beverage can coolies (I sell *tons* of them). What made his order unique was the slogan printed on them and the way he used them to leverage more social media interaction. The coolies were printed with his contact information and the slogan "Stick with the man who covers your can." When Josh received his order, he snapped a photo of the coolies and posted it to social media inviting people to stop by his office for a free beverage coolie. His social media post blew up with reactions, which created numerous opportunities for Josh to interact with prospects and customers. Additionally, Josh created more social media buzz by getting recipients of the coolies to tag him on social media showing how Josh was "covering their can" wherever the recipient happened to be.

24. Marked-up calendar magnets show customers supply delivery dates.

Taylor-Tharp Water Treatment in Bradford, Pennsylvania, schedules routine supply deliveries for the water treatment equipment they sell to homeowners. Every customer receives a calendar magnet marked with a black dot on each date the company will be delivering the water treatment system supplies. The water treatment systems require fresh supplies every eight weeks, and the calendar magnet is an effective way to remind the customer of those delivery dates. Should

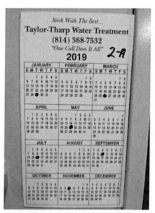

the customer need to call Taylor-Tharp for any reason, the magnet has the company's contact information readily available. Archie Taylor, owner, has been successfully using this technique for over thirty years.

Taylor-Tharp Calendar Magnet

25., 26. Making customers feel appreciated using welcome kits.

Chris Langille, founder and CEO of Advisor Evolved, an internet marketing and web development company, makes new customers feel special by sending them a welcome kit after they've hired his firm. Shortly after becoming a new customer, Advisor Evolved ships out a custom-printed box that contains two pens, a smartphone stand, a backpack, and a T-shirt. All the items are quality, fun, and functional so they'll be used by the recipient and seen by others. They are printed with the company logo so the Advisor Evolved brand will be reinforced over and over again. While I was collecting the information about the welcome kits, Chris pointed out that his customers love receiving them and the kits help solidify the relationship between his company and his customers.

The summer rental business in the resort town of Cape May, New Jersey, is very competitive because there are many realty companies in that market. The realtors are seeking two uniquely different customers: homeowners of available rental properties and renters for those homes. Once the realtor acquires a customer, it's imperative to keep them because they are so difficult to replace. Dagmer Chew, owner of Homestead Real Estate in Cape May, utilizes two different welcome kits to help with customer retention. The first kit is for the homeowners. Once a homeowner contracts with Homestead Real Estate, they receive a quality recyclable grocery tote containing useful items. Inside the tote is a beautiful book about Cape May, two T-shirts, a few pens, and lip balms. These items are useful, which will keep the Homestead Real Estate logo and contact information in front of the homeowner every time they use one of the items.

The rental customer receives the same grocery tote. Some of the items it contains are the same as the homeowner welcome kit, but some of the additional items are more appropriate for someone on vacation. The renter receives a small bucket and shovel, lip balm, pen, bottle opener, lanyards for keys, and a smaller, zippered bag, which can be used for bringing items to the beach. Also included is information about local restaurants and things to do. The items in this welcome kit will be used by the renter during the course of their stay, reinforcing Homestead Real Estate's message, which may encourage the renter to rent through Homestead the following summer.

Advisor Evolved Welcome Kit

Homestead Real Estate's
Homeowner's Welcome Kit

Homestead Real Estate's
Renter's Welcome Kit

27. T-shirt marketing success: resonating with a target market creates branding magic.

The key to successful marketing with T-shirts is to create artwork that appeals to the intended target market. This will encourage them to wear the T-shirts, and this reinforces the branding. In 1994, Vince and Deardra Murphy, owners of Accu-Fire Fabrication, Inc. of Morrisville, Pennsylvania, developed a character named "Accu-Fire Man" as a way to build brand recognition and remind their customers of their quality work and timely delivery. Their company fabricates overhead sprinkler systems for commercial and residential buildings. Their customers are sprinkler installation contractors and their installers. The Accu-Fire Man character is a hard-working, muscle-bound guy with a big smile and who almost always has a pretty lady on his arm. In more than a dozen different designs, Accu-Fire Man appears on the back of the shirts along with entertaining ad copy relevant to the industry. Over twenty-five years later, the T-shirts remain a big hit. They are distributed on the jobsites by the drivers of their delivery trucks. According to the Murphys, when the delivery drivers show up to a jobsite, the installers make a beeline to the delivery truck in order to get a shirt. The installers are required to wear safety colors, and the Accu-Fire shirts are safety green, so they are often seen on the jobsite. Lastly, the shirts are also distributed by Accu-Fire's salespeople when they make sales calls as a way of creating an opportunity to see customers.

28. Spinning prize wheels generate trade show leads.

If you display at trade shows and events, you know firsthand how expensive it can be. Not only do you have to take time out of the office to be there, but there are fees for the booth space and the preparation ahead of the event; the cost of the trade show booth, promotional products, and other marketing collateral; and the salary of any employees who join you. If you walk away from that event with very few or no leads, it's a total waste of time and money.

Aime DeWees of White Insurance & Associates in Charleston, West Virginia, and John Hefferon of Southern Hills Insurance Agency, Inc. in Honeoye, New York, use a similar technique to draw people to their booth and collect leads. They both use spinning prize wheels.

Here's how it works: Small, inexpensive promotional products like jar openers, lip balm, hand sanitizer, and water bottles are purchased as prizes. The name of each item is printed on each of the panels of the prize wheel. The spinning wheel and the noise it generates attracts passersby to the booth. In order to spin the wheel and win a prize, a passerby provides some basic information on a postcard. Some folks request not to be contacted, and of course, their wishes are respected. Next, the person spins the wheel and wins the prize.

Here's why this idea is brilliant: handing out items to anyone who passes by your booth can be expensive and a waste of your marketing money. Making people "earn" your promo items by asking them to give you something in return, like filling out the postcard, will generate more leads for you. Lastly, even if the person does not complete the postcard, gives you false information, or requests that you do not contact them, you still get an opportunity to interact with them before they spin the wheel.

John Hefferon's Trade Show Table
with Spinning Prize Wheel

29. A "better than a business card" business card

If you're like most folks in the business world, you have received hundreds of business cards over the course of your career. If you're like me, you put them in your desk and there they hide. You don't see them again until the next time you clean out your desk. Sadly, this is what happens to the business cards you hand out.

Here's an idea to make sure your business cards don't wind up buried in someone's desk or junk drawer. Karen Kudrna, owner of Kehl Insurance Shoppe in Berwick, Pennsylvania, distributes LintCards™ to her customers and prospects. The card is about the size of a credit card, so it's a bit bigger than a business card, which helps it stand out. It's made of a hard plastic and it's printed in full color on one side with her marketing message. On the opposite side is lint brush fabric that removes lint and debris from clothing. The cards are durable and reusable, so recipients can use them over and over. Do you think the recipients of Karen's LintCards™ find them useful and keep them handy? You bet! Do you think the LintCards™ are buried in a desk or junk drawer? Not a chance!

Many of my customers have purchased another product that is also a unique business card. They buy custom-printed microfiber cloths and have them folded and inserted into clear vinyl pouches. These cloths are used to clean eyeglasses and sunglasses, smartphones, and any other device that has a screen. The microfiber cloths are available in many sizes, but most are about 6x6. When folded into the clear vinyl pouch, they are roughly the size of a business card and can be distributed as such. Both the Lintcard™ and the microfiber cloths have a much higher perceived value when compared to the typical business card because they are useful and recipients will hold on to them longer.

On a personal note, a car dealership local to me has an unbelievable offer for car detailing. I'm assuming it's a loss leader to attract people to the dealership for repairs and service, since the price is so low. I take my car there twice a year to be detailed and every time I pick up my car, a microfiber cloth folded in a pouch is resting on my console. I have many suppliers for this item and I receive samples of this item regularly, but oddly enough, every time I receive a new microfiber cloth from the dealership, I appreciate it. That little extra makes me feel as if they have completed a thorough job and that they want to impress upon me that attention to detail is important to them.

30. Using whoopee cushions to make some noise.

Barry and Mark Burkholder, owners of Burkholder, a landscape design and maintenance firm located in Malvern, Pennsylvania, sponsored and participated in the Chili Cook-off in Chester County. They wanted to do a promotional product that was connected with eating chili, so they chose to purchase whoopee cushions. The whoopee cushions were imprinted with the Burkholder logo, website, phone number, and the name of their chili, which was "Blow-Out Chili." The whoopee cushions were a huge hit. Event attendees were flocking to their table to get one. Folks were having a great time with them, as the sound they generate could be heard throughout the event. Burkholder wound up receiving some additional marketing at no charge. The whoopee cushions drew the attention of a local radio host, who interviewed Barry's daughter on air.

Burkholder's Whoopee Cushion

31. A beer mug brings business.

My customer Barry Burkholder is an avid runner, and his company sponsored a local charity race. His sponsorship included beer mugs printed with his company logo and contact information, which were used at an event party scheduled after the race. Months later, a recipient of one of the mugs hired

Burkholder to do a $35,000 project at his home. The new customer made it a point to tell Barry that he called Burkholder as a result of receiving the beer mug, and he used the information found on the mug to contact hm.

32. T-Shirts for Tots

Barry and Mark Burkholder noticed that they often have an audience when they do a residential project. Young kids, especially boys, love watching the heavy equipment dig into dirt and stone, so they chose to have some kids' T-shirts printed to give away on the jobsite. On the front, the shirts were printed with an image of a backhoe and the words "I dig Burkholder . . ." in a font that looks like kids' handwriting. On the back, it was printed with the Burkholder logo and the words ". . . and so will you."

After one specific project was completed, Barry had a follow-up visit with the customer two weeks later. The homeowner told him her son loved the T-shirt so much, he refused to take it off. The appropriate messaging on the shirt and the connection between the boy and the fun he had watching Barry's crew work was so strong that the boy insisted on wearing the shirt, which delivered Burkholder's message over and over.

33. Market your business with custom-printed stadium cushions.

One of my insurance agent customers came up with an idea that could work for just about any business that markets to the local community. He ordered custom-printed stadium cushions and then donated them to the high school booster club as a fundraiser.

Here's how it worked: First, he contacted the booster club and made arrangements to donate the stadium cushions. Then he ordered them. The stadium cushions were printed on one side with his contact information and a catchy slogan that read, "We Protect Important Assets." On the opposite side, an image of the high school mascot and "Go Patriots!" was printed. Upon delivery, the booster club could then sell the stadium cushions for whatever price they wanted and keep all the money for the club.

34. Show school spirit with plastic footballs and basketballs.

Over the years, I've had several of my customers sponsor either the football booster club or the basketball booster club. The sponsorship allowed them to have custom-printed plastic footballs or basketballs printed with their contact information, which were then thrown into the crowd by the cheerleaders. The folks in the stands would catch the balls and keep them as keepsakes.

35. A creative key tag idea

I've literally sold millions of key tags during my career, but it wasn't until the spring of 2018 that I heard of the most *brilliant* of ideas using custom-printed key tags. Whenever Mike Summers of Summers Insurance in Mishawaka, Indiana, sells a homeowner's policy, he gives his new customer a key tag. He then suggests that the customer write their name on the back of the key tag and put a spare key on the ring. The customer could then give the spare key to a friend, neighbor, or relative so they could get into their house in the event of an emergency.

He then points out that his information is on the key tag in case the recipient of the spare key needs him for any reason. This idea is amazingly simple and clever!

36. Promotional calendars can generate repeat business.

Custom-printed calendars are still effective even though they are one of the oldest forms of promotional products. Their value is tough to beat because they are typically inexpensive, and when distributed to customers, they deliver a marketing message month after month for a year for less than pennies each day. Joe Vansant, owner of JV Auto Service in Wilmington, Delaware, uses calendars to earn more service work from his existing customer base. His distribution method costs him absolutely nothing; he has the calendars available for his customers at his counter for them to take, or his service staff leave them in the customers' cars. He has been distributing calendars for so many years that his customers have come to rely on Joe for their annual calendar. Year after year, his customers will call or stop by asking for next year's calendar, which gives him an opportunity to talk to them and discuss needed service work or to schedule an appointment for maintenance. The service work generated by these interactions is well worth his annual investment.

37., 38. Creative T-shirt ad copy gets attention.

When a marketer purchases T-shirts, the most important objective is to entice recipients to wear them, otherwise the money spent on them is wasted. This makes sense, right? In order to accomplish this objective, shirts need to either have a catchy design, logo, or slogan, or the shirt itself must be special in some way. One of my insurance customers hit the ball out of the park by printing "Call My Agent" on the front of baseball-style T-shirts and then had her contact information printed on the back. Baseball shirts are not the typical T-shirt in that they have three-quarter-length sleeves that are a different color than the body of the shirt. The slogan and shirt are eye catching and unique, which could start a conversation. The shirts were distributed to recipients at her office. She took an extra step to generate more leads by posting on social media a photo of two of her employees modeling the shirts with the message that folks could stop by her office for a free T-shirt. Then she took a further step by buying pens incorporating the "Call My Agent" slogan, which were distributed around her town.

A pizza chain in my area uses creative ad copy on its employees' T-shirts. The T-shirts are black with a multicolor print on the back that reads, "Legalize Marinara." I must admit, the first time I saw this, I did a double take and got a chuckle from it. The slogan is memorable and fun, and I'm sure it sparks interactions between the customers and employees of the company.

39. Coupon pens generate repeat business.

Several years ago, I was staying at a hotel for a few days, and one evening I decided to get a pizza for dinner, which I would eat in my room. Near the hotel was the location of a well-known pizza chain, and I walked over and ordered something to go. As I was checking out, the counter person handed me a pen along with my pizza. The ad copy on the pen included a small discount coupon for all to-go orders. The terms of the coupon were clearly printed on the pen, but the counter person explained how to use the coupon. In order to get the discount, a pizza buyer has to order a pizza for takeout between Sunday and Wednesday, and the buyer must bring the pen into the store and show the pen to the cashier when picking up the order. The cashier would then apply the discount at checkout. As a person who markets his owns business and who sells marketing, this piqued my curiosity, and I asked the counter person more about the coupon pen. As it turns out, the weekend is the busiest part of the week for the restaurant, and Sunday through Wednesday is the slowest. The pens are only distributed to customers on Thursdays, Fridays, and Saturdays, and because the coupon is not valid on those days, the customer must come back on a slow day to take advantage of the discount. Also, the coupon on the pen has an expiration date, which encourages returning customers to come back for a new pen after the coupon expires.

At the basic level, the coupon generates sales on slower days, but it accomplishes much more than that. Here's why this idea is amazingly brilliant: When a customer uses the coupon to buy another pizza, the cost to acquire that additional sale is the small discount on the pizza. Also, since the customer needs to show the pen to the cashier, the customer needs to keep the pen and replace it when the coupon expires. During the valid time period, the ad copy on the pen creates many impressions on the customer. Lastly, the coupon can influence a future buying decision. The customer may choose that company's pizza over other foods (including other pizza companies) simply because they have a coupon.

40. Cooking magnets kept in kitchen

My mother-in-law is an amazing cook. Just about every Sunday, my wife and I make a short drive to her home for a gourmet dinner. I don't recall seeing her use a cookbook, so she must have the recipes ingrained into her brain. However, hanging on her refrigerator is a reference tool that may aid her in creating her delicacies. This reference tool is a 5x7 magnet printed with cooking equivalents. For example, three teaspoons equal one tablespoon. She uses this information to adjust her recipes depending on how much food she's making for dinner. Printed at the bottom of the magnet is ad copy for a local company, and she sees that marketing message every time she looks at the magnet. The magnet has been hanging on her fridge for over a decade.

41. You can bank on pizza cutters.

A banker was promoting lines of credit to local businesses. Her bank had a simple application process that was unique to her bank, and she thought it would help her get more appointments with decision makers. She made phone call after phone call with little success, so she decided to take a different tack in order to increase the number of appointments. She purchased quality pizza cutters imprinted with her name and the name of the bank. She wrote a sales letter that featured ad copy that played off the pizza cutter. She explained that her bank's application process is so easy it cuts through the hassles and red tape normally associated with getting a line of credit. The letter and the pizza cutter were inserted into a box, and she mailed them a few at a time to her prospects. When she called to follow up, she told the recipient she was the person who sent the pizza cutter, and this facilitated a conversation, which often led to an appointment. According to my source, her appointment rate doubled as a result of her pizza cutter mailing.

42. Car buyers are fans of foldable fans.

If you were walking through a car lot in the middle of summer, you might get a bit hot, right? The sun beating down on the asphalt might make it feel like you're standing on the sun. A car dealership in Ohio came up with a creative way to welcome prospects to their dealership. They purchased foldable hand fans printed with the dealership name and contact info. When prospects are seen walking out on the lot, a salesperson greets them and asks if they have questions or need help. The salesperson then gives the fans to the prospects and encourages them to use the fans as they browse. This idea is so smart for a number of reasons: First, the foldable fan is useful, and the prospect will most likely keep the fan. This is the type of item you'll never know you need one until you need one. Next, how many dealerships hand out foldable hand fans? It's unlikely that another dealership in the area is doing the same thing, and this makes that dealership unique. The fans may remind the prospects of their visit if they move on to another dealership. This could help keep that dealership in consideration during the buying process.

43. Umbrellas create a downpour of advertising.

When you travel, do you pack an umbrella? Most likely you don't, but one high-end hotel has their guests covered in the event of drizzly weather. They keep a supply of custom-printed umbrellas at the front desk for their guests to use. When the weather turns rainy, the guests can stay dry when they leave the hotel and go about their business. Some of the guests return the umbrellas, and some guests keep them. A quality umbrella is not inexpensive, and they have a high perceived value, leaving the guest with a positive impression about the hotel. Every time the guest uses the umbrella, the hotel's branding is seen many times, as the useful life of an umbrella can last for years.

A FINAL WORD

Git-r-done!

—Larry the Cable Guy

My next-door neighbor's house was featured on one of those home improvement shows. I'm sure you're familiar with the concept: a construction crew descends upon a nice family's house, tears it up, and puts it back together in thirty minutes. I can assure you their house took a lot longer than thirty minutes to put back together—it took about six weeks from beginning to end.

This is the perfect metaphor for marketing. Successful marketing takes time, effort, patience, and creativity. Don't expect your marketing to be an overnight success. If you do experience immediate success, BRAVO! You should celebrate, but don't be discouraged if it takes longer than you expect.

I heard a saying that goes like this: "The best time to plant a tree is twenty years ago, and today." Marketing is no different. If you haven't made the effort to market your business, start today and keep doing it consistently. Success will eventually come. You'll probably make some mistakes along the way, but don't give up.

Marketing is both a science and an art. The founder of Guerrilla Marketing, Jay Conrad Levinson, says, "Consistency breeds familiarity, familiarity breeds confidence, and confidence breeds sales."[10] When it comes time for a customer or prospect to make a purchase, a transaction will occur only when the buyer feels comfortable. A comfortable customer is a happy customer who will gladly buy from you again and refer others to you.

I once heard someone say that people buy emotionally; they don't buy intellectually. Buyers want to feel safe when they part with their money.

---

[10] Jay Conrad Levinson, *Guerrilla Marketing: Easy and Inexpensive Strategies for Making Big Profits from Your Small Business* (New York: Houghton Mifflin Company, 2007). Originally published in 1983.

Buyers want to feel as if they are making a square deal and that they are not squandering their investment. They want to feel that their buying decision fulfills some unmet need. Buyer's remorse is the kiss of death for any marketer, and eliminating it is of the highest importance. Their confidence in your brand is imperative, and this confidence is built through effective messaging. Everything from your product or service to how you answer your phone to your email signature to your logo, even the colors in your logo, says something about your brand. Any point of contact you have with your customers and prospects, no matter how minute, creates an impression about your company. This is the essence of marketing.

The unique nature of promotional products makes them a powerful marketing medium because they can create a physical and emotional connection between the marketer and the buyer. The ability for promotional products to be accepted into the lives of your customers and prospects, and the way they keep delivering your message without interruption or additional cost, is unmatched by any other marketing medium.

When a customer or prospect is exposed to your marketing message repeatedly, it will create a level of comfort. This fosters familiarity, confidence, and ultimately sales, as Mr. Levinson explains. Then, when you factor in the lifetime value of your customers (including referrals), the profits you reap over time make your marketing investment look like chump change.

Thank you for taking the time to read my book. I sure hope it will help you make more money and help you achieve your goals.

Happy marketing!

PS: If you have a promotional product success story or a unique way of using them, I'd love to hear about it.

Feel free to email me at info@mankocompany.com.

FREE THIRTY-MINUTE MARKETING CONSULTATION

After reading this book, you may have questions about promotional products. I'd be happy to help you. It's my way of saying thank you for reading my book.

Feel free to contact me and schedule your thirty-minute consultation about promotional products or anything marketing related. This consultation will be at no charge to you.

You can reach me at info@mankocompany.com.

I look forward to hearing from you!

Avery

Avery Manko has been involved in sales, marketing, and entrepreneurship since 1990, with his primary focus being promotional products marketing. His company, The Manko Company, is a promotional products distributorship. They've helped thousands of businesses throughout the United States build their brand, get more leads and referrals, retain customers, and increase sales. Avery and his wife, Diana, live in Wilmington, Delaware, with their chihuahua, Daisy.